Excel® Power Presentations

Excel® Power Presentations

Stephen L. Nelson

Addison-Wesley Publishing Company

Reading, Massachusetts   Menlo Park, California   New York
Don Mills, Ontario   Wokingham, England   Amsterdam   Bonn
Sydney   Singapore   Tokyo   Madrid   San Juan
Paris   Seoul   Milan   Mexico City   Taipei

Library of Congress Cataloging-in-Publication Data

Nelson, Stephen L., 1959-
    Excel power presentations : high-impact graphics that make you look good / Steve Nelson.
       p.   cm.
    Includes index.
    ISBN 0-201-63294-2
    1. Microsoft Excel (Computer file) 2. Business--Computer programs. 3. ElectRonic spreadsheetS. I. Title.
    HF5548.4.M523N452 1992
    001.4'226'02855369--dc20   92-36799
                                              CIP

Managing Editor: Amorette Pedersen
Set in 10.5-point Palatino by Benchmark Productions

1 2 3 4 5 6 7 8 9-DO-9695949392
First Printing, November, 1992

Contents

Contents

Contents

Contents

Contents

Introduction

My first experience creating a computer-generated chart was, well, a disaster. I was new on the job—I think it might even have been my first day. The boss, busy with a board of directors meeting, wanted a quick chart that plotted demand curves for our company's product along with the demand curves for several of our competitors' products.

"So far, so good," I remember thinking to myself. I knew what a demand curve was. I figured that somebody around the office had colored pencils and a good ruler.

Then, before I even had a chance to ask about graph paper, the boss said something terrifying, "We've got that new Lotus program. I think you can do this with that."

I won't bore you with the tedious details of the two hours that followed, but I never did get Lotus 1-2-3 to produce the chart.

Part of the problem, it turned out, was that Lotus 1-2-3 couldn't and still can't do what I needed it to do. (Excel, by the way, can.) But the major problem was that it was my first experience with Lotus 1-2-3 and I didn't have the skills needed to accomplish the job. As a result, I ended up looking more than just a little foolish. Worse, however, was that the board of directors and management chose a pricing structure that played a major role in the company's ultimate failure.

I know you're not interested in my life story, but there are a couple of lessons one can glean from my demand-curve debacle. The first lesson is that if you're creating a chart for the first time or if you're only going to create charts infrequently, it's easy to waste time and energy creating charts. So, to make sure that you never waste time and energy creating your charts—or worse yet, fail—this book describes, in step-by-step fashion, exactly how to quickly create each of Excel's 13 basic chart types. (In fact, using the chart templates on the accompanying disk, you can create charts in about 15 seconds.)

The book also explains when these charts are and are not appropriate.

There's also a second, more subtle lesson that can be learned from the demand-curve debacle, though. Graphical representations of data, or data graphics, are extremely powerful tools for revealing and communicating data. And you'll make better decisions in the work you do—whatever it happens to be—if you exploit the awesome power of good data graphics. In the case of the demand-curve chart, I'm not saying a snazzy chart plotting demand curves would have made the company successful. But with a revealing data graphic, the board of directors and senior management would have better understood the pricing of our competitors and implemented a more competitive pricing structure for our products. And who knows what might have happened then . . .

Using This Book

You're probably anxious to get into the meat of things, but let me give you some information that will make it easier: specifically, how this book is organized, what I assume you already know about Excel, and a little bit about me so you can put the information and opinions contained in this book into proper perspective.

How This Book Is Organized

You'll find it helpful if you understand how this book is organized. Then you'll know where to turn if you want information on a particular topic. This book is organized into seven chapters:

- *Chapter 1, **Charting Fundamentals,** explains what charts are and how they plot worksheet data, how you use the ChartWizard to create charts in Excel, and how you print and save the charts you create. Chapter 1 also describes how you create charts using the templates on the disk that accompanies this book.*

- *Chapter 2, **Simple Charts,** describes how you create charts from scratch. Chapter 2 also describes the strengths, weaknesses, and design issues related to using Excel's two-dimensional area, bar, column, line, and pie charts. In addition, it includes the names of the two-dimensional area, bar, column, line, and pie chart templates, and illustrates each of them with a figure.*

- *Chapter 3, **Advanced Charts,** describes the strengths, weaknesses, and design issues related to using Excel's combination, xy, and radar charts, as well as its three-dimensional area, bar, column, line, pie, and surface charts. In addition, Chapter 3 includes the names of templates for these chart types and illustrates each one with a figure.*

- *Chapter 4, **Drawing,** is a short chapter. It explains how you access Excel's drawing tools, and how you use these drawing tools to change the appearance of Excel charts.*

- *Chapter 5, **Customizing Your Charts,** describes how you change the way your Excel charts look by doing things like adding to and editing the plotted data series, changing the color of various chart parts, and modifying the calibration of chart axes. In short, you can change just about any aspect of an Excel chart, and Chapter 5 tells you how.*

- *Chapter 6, **Working with Excel,** describes Excel application issues that relate indirectly to charting, including such things as the steps for creating custom document color palettes, how to use the Spelling command to verify the spelling of text used in a chart, how and why you protect and recalculate chart documents, and how to perform graphical problem solving by adjusting data markers.*

- *Chapter 7, **Producing Chart Output,** goes into more detail about how you successfully produce chart output with Excel. It describes what happens when you print both black-and-white and color versions of Excel charts, how to mitigate some of the problems you're likely to encounter, how to produce 35mm slides, how to create on-line "slide shows" that the Excel application runs for you, and how to use object linking and embedding.*

There's one other thing I want to mention here, too. The editors created a solid, working index. Remember it's there. If you have a question about some menu command or product feature, the index usually provides the fastest method for locating the page on which a particular topic is discussed.

What You Need to Know

This isn't a book about Windows. So, while I don't assume you're some kind of Windows expert, I do assume you know your way around the Windows operating environment. For example, I assume you know how to start and stop Windows and Windows applications like Excel. I assume you know how to choose commands from menus and how to work the various elements of windows and dialog boxes such as entering data into text boxes and marking and unmarking check boxes. If you don't know how to do these sorts of things, you'll find it extremely beneficial to learn more about Windows before you begin your charting. To acquire this knowledge, you can read the introductory sections of the Windows user documentation. You can also purchase and then read one of the many Windows tutorials.

You don't actually need to know very much about Excel to use this book. Nevertheless, you still need to know a few things. You should know how to enter data—labels, values, and formulas—into worksheet cells. You should know how to cut, copy, paste, and clear data. And you should understand the difference between the Excel application, or program, window and the document windows Excel uses to display things like the worksheets and charts you create. None of this information is difficult to acquire if you don't already possess it. The Excel documentation does a good job of explaining how to construct worksheets. Or, you can pick up an Excel tutorial from a local bookstore.

A Few Words About the Author

If you read the available literature on data graphics, you quickly realize that there are two distinct philosophies about the place and purpose of data graphics. One group sees data graphics as visual gimmicks you can use to spice up things like lengthy reports or boring magazine articles. The other group sees data graphics as tools you use to reveal the truths otherwise hidden or obfuscated in the details of the data.

Mentioning this polarization may seem like a funny digression—particularly here at the very beginning of the book. After all, you haven't even seen a chart yet. But I have a reason for bringing up the subject here. You have a right to know from the very start which philosophy I adhere to.

Here are a few things you should know about me so you can put the information contained in the pages that follow—especially those comments I've identified as my opinion—in perspective. In a nutshell, I'm a data analyst who focuses on the analysis and presentation of quantitative information. And, in my work, my responsibilities have revolved around the analysis and communication of quantitative, usually financial, information.

Because I'm a data analyst, this book focuses on how you use data graphics as tools for understanding and effectively communicating information. So, you aren't going to get information in this book on the aesthetic qualities of various fonts, but you will learn which fonts increase readability. Similarly, you won't get my ideas as to which colors are in fashion this season, but you will read about which color combinations create problems for people with color blindness. And while I'll explain how you go about creating every Excel chart type, I'll also point out which types—such as three-dimensional pie charts—should never, ever, be used, and why. To sum up, the design issues I'll address here will focus on things you should know to make your charts powerful and successful communication tools—not pop art.

1

Charting Fundamentals

If you've worked with Excel's charts before and feel comfortable creating, printing, and saving charts, you can skip this chapter. You don't need the information it provides. On the other hand, if you haven't felt comfortable doing these things or if you've always felt a little vague about terms like *data series* and *data points*, take the time to peruse the following pages.

To start, I'll give you a quick primer on how Excel views the data it charts so you know how to organize the worksheet data. Then, I'll explain how to use Excel's ChartWizard to create snappy looking charts in record time and how to print and save the charts you create. At the end of the chapter, I'll also introduce you to some of the subtleties of chart design so your creations will look professional.

What Excel Charts

Excel graphs numeric data you've stored in an Excel worksheet. Therefore, the very first thing you need to do if you're going to chart using Excel is to enter the data or possibly calculate the data using the spreadsheet. I'm not going to describe how you enter data into a spreadsheet here. I assume you already know how to do that. If you don't, the Excel documentation does a good job of explaining how you construct Excel worksheets. Or, you can also acquire one of the many Excel tutorials—probably from the same bookstore where you purchased this book. (For what it's worth, I like Doug Cobb's *Running Excel*, from Microsoft Press.)

Understanding Data Series and Points

Even after you've entered the data you want to graph into a spreadsheet, you need to understand how Excel views and interprets that data. Specifically, you need to understand the difference between data series and data points.

To provide a backdrop against which to have this discussion, I've created the worksheet shown in Figure 1-1. It shows fictitious bauxite production for Argentina, Brazil, and Chile over a 5-year period, including both actual and estimated mining activity. (Bauxite, by the way, is the principal ore of aluminum.) Figure 1-2 shows the same data as Figure 1-1 in a simple column chart.

Later in the chapter, I'll describe how to use the data shown in Figure 1-1 to create the bar chart shown in Figure 1-2. But for now, just concentrate on the concepts and not the mechanics.

Each of the individual pieces of data that will be graphed is called a data point. The value 35,000 in cell B2, for example, is a data point; it is shown as the first red column in the chart in Figure 1-2. The value 45,000 in cell B3 is another data point; it is shown as the first green column in the chart.

A collection of related data points is a data series. For example, the Argentinean bauxite numbers in row 2 is one data series. The Brazilian bauxite numbers in row 3 is another data series. The Chilean bauxite numbers in row 4 is a third data series. On a color monitor or printer, Excel identifies data series with color. In Figure 1-2, Excel uses the color red for each of the bars representing the Argentinean data series, green for the Brazilian data series, and blue for the Chilean data series. On a monochrome monitor, Excel uses different cross-hatching patterns, or shades of gray.

Figure 1-1: Ficti-
tious South
American baux-
ite-production
data.

Figure 1-2: A sim-
ple column chart.
This chart
illustrates the
difference
between data
points (single
values) and data
series (a collec-
tion of related
data points).

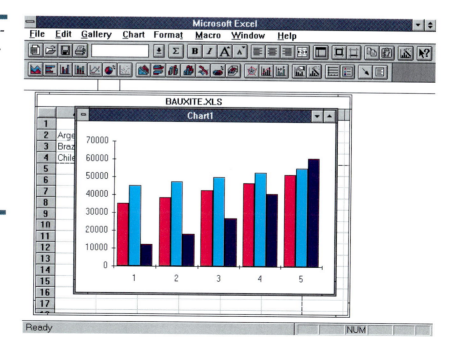

Some charts only show a single data series. For example, if you only wanted to show Argentinean bauxite production, you would only have a single data series. When you do only have a single data series, you can use different colors for each of the data points.

Series Names and Category Names

It's not an absolute requirement, but you'll find it useful to name data series; you can do so just by entering an appropriate label into the worksheet storing the data. These names can be used later to either label the columns or to create legends that identify which colors represent which data series. In Figure 1-1, cell A2 holds the label "Argentina," so you might decide to use it as a label for the Argentinean bauxite production data series. In a similar fashion, the labels "Brazil" and "Chile" might be used to label the Brazilian and Chilean bauxite production data series. Figure 1-3 shows the same column chart as Figure 1-2, except that a legend appears to the right of the chart.

In most cases, you will also categorize the data points. Categories simply describe the data points within each of the data series. In Figure 1-1, for example, the value 1, which identifies the first year, is the first data point category. Value 2 is the second data point category. Values 3, 4, and 5 are the third, fourth, and fifth data point categories.

Data categories are used to describe the various sets of data points. Notice in Figures 1-2 and 1-3, for example, how the year numbers or data category names appear beneath each of the sets of columns.

There is a limit to the number of data series you can fit in a chart and the number of data points you can fit in a data series. A chart can't have more than 255 data series. A data series can't have more than 4,000 data points. These limits,

Figure 1-3: A column chart with a legend. This column chart has a legend at the right.

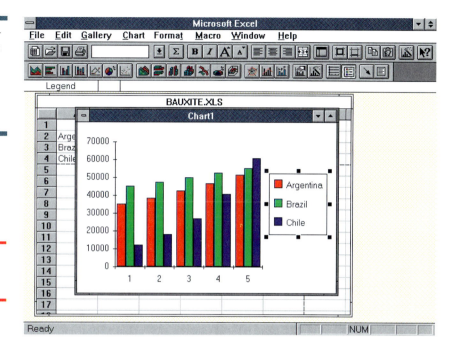

Tip!

The data-series and data-point limits mean that for large data sets you'll want to arrange your data series into rows rather than columns, because an Excel worksheet provides only 256 columns, but 16,384 rows.

which are heads above the series and point limits of the other popular spreadsheet programs, should cause no problem for the vast majority of users. I should say, however, that the number of data series and data points in a chart greatly affects the speed with which Excel draws the chart. On my 80386, which runs at 33mhz and has 8 megabytes of memory, a chart with a single data series of 400 points takes almost forever to draw, or so it seems.

Technical Tip

Data Series Versus Data Categories

This business about data series and data categories can get confusing. The reason for the confusion, however, has nothing to do with your basic intelligence. If you're confused by these two terms (I admit that I was), your confusion stems from the fact that series and categories are simply different ways to slice the same data set. So, when you get right down to it, the definitions are arbitrary. If you are most concerned with national bauxite production, your data series are the rows of national bauxite production data and your data categories are years. If you were most concerned with the annual South American bauxite product, your data series would be the annual-production data, and your data categories would be countries. In other words, the data series just describe the dominant views of the data you want to chart.

Let me give you one other tip regarding series and category confusion. If you're creating a time-series chart, which is simply a chart that tracks a particular variable over time, a time-based unit of measurement such as months or years will never be your data series definition; it will always be your category.

The Parts of Charts

To make it easier to describe and discuss Excel's charts, we need to work with a common set of definitions. I've already described one important chart part—the legend—but there are half-a-dozen other terms for which we need to use a common definition.

Data Markers

Data markers are the graphical representations used to chart individual data points. In Figures 1-2 and 1-3, Excel uses individual columns to represent data points. There are more than

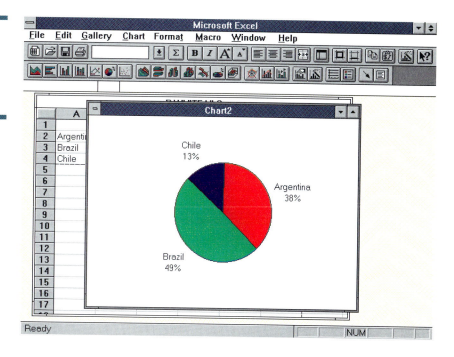

Figure 1-4: A pie chart. This pie chart uses pie-slice data markers.

half-a-dozen data-marker varieties, however. In Figure 1-4, Excel uses the slices of a pie chart as data markers. (A pie chart only charts a single data series.) In Figure 1-5, Excel uses small, colored squares, which happen to be connected with lines, as data markers. Figure 1-5 is called a line chart.

Figures 1-3, 1-4, and 1-5 illustrate three of the basic Excel chart types: a column chart, a pie chart, and a line chart. However, Excel provides many more chart types—13 in all. Chapter 2 and Chapter 3 describe and detail each chart type.

Data-Marker Descriptions

To describe and calibrate data markers, Excel uses scales and labels. You're probably already familiar with both graphic elements, so I'll make the ensuing discussion brief. Scales, as you may know, are simply the vertical and horizontal axes that identify categories and quantify the data markers. In Figures

Figure 1-5: A line chart. Here, squares are used as data markers.

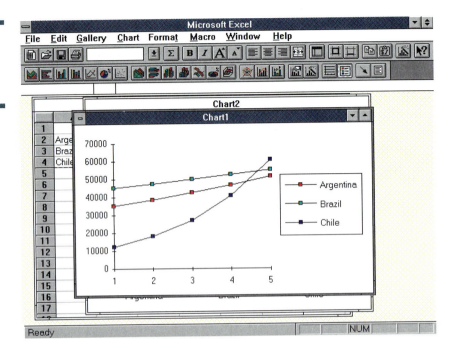

1-2 and 1-3, for example, the vertical axis, which is called a Y-axis, calibrates the plotted data-point values. The horizontal axis, which is called an X-axis, describes the data categories (1, 2, 3, and so on). Using these two axes, you can more quickly identify specific data points, and you can visually gauge the underlying data-point values. The first year's bauxite production for Argentina, for example, is 35,000. You use the Y-axis to calibrate the data-point values; you use the X-axis scale to find the various years' data points.

Labels describe specific data points. In the pie chart in Figure 1-4, the slices of the pie are described two ways: with textual labels that identify the categories and with percentage labels that express the underlying data-point value as a percentage of the total of all the data-point values. (Remember, a pie chart shows only a single data series.) You can also label data points

Figure 1-6: A column chart with value labels.

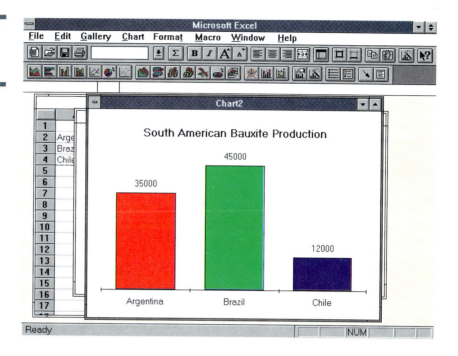

with the actual data-point values themselves, as shown in Figure 1-6. Note that Figure 1-6 doesn't include a value axis; with the labeled data points, one isn't needed.

Chart Titles and Text

You can add a textual description to any chart, which means you can identify the charted data or point out information that chart reveals. Figure 1-6, as you might have noticed, shows the title, "South American Bauxite Production." Excel also lets you add textual titles to the Y- and X-axis scales, and it lets you add text anywhere on the chart. I'll talk more about annotating charts with text in Chapter 5, *Customizing Charts*.

Plot Area and Chart Areas

Two other chart terms you need to understand are plot area and chart area. The *plot area* is the part of the chart that shows a chart's data markers and data-marker descriptions. In the column chart in Figure 1-6, the rectangle that shows the columns, scales, and data labels is the plot area. In the pie chart in Figure 1-4, the circle that shows the pie slices and the data labels that identify the pie slices comprise the plot area.

The chart window interior you see in Figure 1-6 is the chart area, including the plot area, the legend if there is one, and any chart titles or text. What you see in Figure 1-6—the rectangular figure that appears on the page—is the chart area.

Working with ChartWizard

With the information you now possess, you'll be well equipped to begin building your charts using the ChartWizard. To illustrate the mechanics of working with ChartWizard, suppose you want to create a column chart that shows South American bauxite production for a 5-year period like the column chart shown in Figure 1-2.

Tip!

When you want to use a chart to communicate a single message, use the message as the chart title. Suppose, for example, your message is that sales are growing, and you've collected 5 years of revenue data to support this message. Rather than label a chart with a description of the data, such as "Five-year sales history," you'll find it most effective to label the chart with the message "Sales continue to grow," thereby focusing viewers on the data that supports your message. (This focusing effect can be particularly important when there are several messages the charted data communicates, and your message isn't the most obvious one.)

To follow along with the step-by-step discussion below, take a minute or so to enter the raw data shown in Figure 1-1. That data is what I'm going to describe how to chart. As you enter the data, be sure to enter the text and values into exactly the same cell locations, as shown in Figure 1-1. Then, once you've entered the raw data you want to chart, take the following steps to chart the data:

Tip!

If you want the chart area to be perfectly square, you can hold down the Shift key as you drag the mouse. To align the chart area with the cells over which you're dragging the mouse, hold down the Alt key as you drag the mouse.

1. Select the worksheet range that holds the data-series names and points and the category names, A1:F4.

2. Click the ChartWizard tool on the Excel Toolbar. The ChartWizard tool is the second tool button from the right end of the Toolbar. On the face of the tool button is a picture of a column chart with what's supposed to be a magic wand. (Wizards, as you know, use magic wands.) When you click the ChartWizard tool, Excel changes the mouse pointer to a cross hair.

3. Drag the mouse from the point you want to be the top-left corner of the chart area to the point you want to be the bottom-right corner of the chart area. When you've identified the desired chart area, release the mouse button. Excel displays the first ChartWizard dialog box, as shown in Figure 1-7.

Figure 1-7: The first Chart-Wizard dialog box.

The first ChartWizard dialog box just prompts you to confirm that the worksheet-range selection contains the data you want to chart, including the series and category names.

4. If you correctly selected the worksheet range in step 2, the range specified in the dialog box's text box will be correct. If you didn't correctly specify the worksheet range, you'll need to correct the range shown. When the

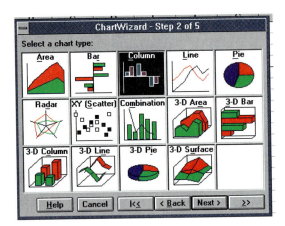

Figure 1-8: The second Chart-Wizard dialog box.

range is correct, select Next to proceed to the next ChartWizard dialog box, which displays the basic Excel chart types (see Figure 1-8).

Besides Next, the ChartWizard dialog boxes provide several other command buttons as well. Help starts the Help application and displays information on the ChartWizard. Cancel stops the ChartWizard. |<< displays the first ChartWizard dialog box. Back displays the previous ChartWizard dialog box, if there is one. And >> skips any remaining ChartWizard dialog boxes and draws the chart using the default settings.

5. Click on the Excel chart type you want to use given your data and the purpose of the chart you're creating: Area, Bar, Column, Line, Pie, Radar, XY, Combination, 3D Area, 3D Bar, 3D Column, 3D Line, 3D Pie, and 3D Surface. When you've selected the desired chart type, click Next; Excel displays the third ChartWizard dialog box, which lists the predefined formats available for the chart type you selected (see Figure 1-9).

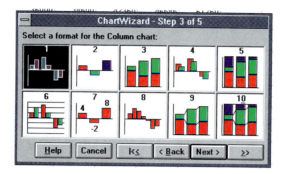

Figure 1-9: The third Chart-Wizard dialog box. This dialog box shows pre-defined formats for chart types.

On page 19, under the heading, "Chart Design Fundamentals," I'll briefly describe when a chart type is and is not appropriate. What's more, the next two chapters describe each of the basic Excel chart types in detail.

6. Each of the chart pictures represents a predefined chart format available for a chart type. You simply click on the chart picture that most closely resembles the way you want your chart to look. Then, when you've selected the desired format, click Next. Excel displays the fourth ChartWizard dialog box, which draws a chart of the type and format you've specified in steps 5 and 6 (see Figure 1-10). You use this dialog box to fix any errors that the ChartWizard made in interpreting the chart-data series, category names, and series names.

7. Excel assumes that your chart data will have more categories than series. So, in the case of the South American bauxite production, Excel assumes that the data series are in rows, because when you exclude series and category names, there are three rows and five columns of actual to-be-charted data. When Excel's assumption isn't correct, you use the Data Series In radio button, set to manually specify how the data series are arranged: by row or by column.

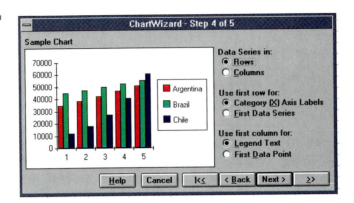

Figure 1-10: The fourth Chart-Wizard dialog box. The fourth dialog box lets you see what your chart looks like thus far with the design decisions you've already made.

8. Excel assumes that the first row in a data-series-by-row selection, or the first column in a data-series-by-column selection, contains category names if the first cell in the row or column is blank. Because of this rule, for example, Excel assumes that row 1 in Figure 1-1 contains category names because cell A1 is blank. When Excel's assumption about data-series arrangement isn't correct, you use the Use First Row For/Use First Column For radio button set to specify whether category names are stored in the first row or column of the selected worksheet range. (Excel changes the name of the second radio button set from Use First Row For to Use First Column For if you've indicated that the data series are arranged by column.)

9. If the column or row contains text, Excel assumes that the first column in a data-series-by-row worksheet selection or the first row in a data-series-by-column worksheet selection stores the data series names. Because of this rule, for example, Excel assumes that column A in Figure 1-1 contains data-series names because cells A2, A3, and A4 hold text. When Excel's assumption isn't correct, you use the Use First Column For/Use First Row For radio button set to specify whether series names are stored in

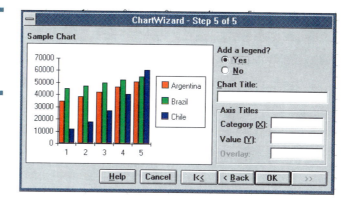

Figure 1-11: The fifth Chart-Wizard dialog box.

the first column or row of the selected worksheet range. (Excel changes the name of the third radio button set from Use First Column For to Use First Row For if you've indicated that the data series are arranged by column.)

10. When the fourth ChartWizard dialog box is correct, select Next. Excel displays the fifth dialog box, as shown in Figure 1-11, which you'll use to complete construction of the chart.

11. (Optional) Use the Add A Legend radio button to specify whether Excel should add a legend using the data series included in the worksheet selection. Predictably, you need to have included the series names in the worksheet selection to be able to use them for a legend.

12. Use the Chart Title text box to specify a title for the chart. To add a particular chart title, such as "South American Bauxite Production," simply type it into the Chart Title text box.

When you're creating a chart for use as a presentation graphic—an overhead transparency, say, or a 35mm slide—the people viewing the chart usually don't have the time or concentration to delve deeply into the data. Therefore, the presentation graphic chart shouldn't show much data—perhaps only one or two data series and not more than a handful of data markers.

13. Use the Axis Titles text boxes to specify titles for the Y- and X-axis scales. To add an X-axis title, such as "Years," type it into the Category (X) text box. To add a Y-axis title, such as "Metric Tons," simply type it into the Value (Y) text box. [The Overlay (Y) axis-title text box labels the second Y-axis of a combination chart with a title. Chapter 3, *Advanced Charts*, describes how and why you create combination charts.]

14. As you use the fifth ChartWizard dialog box to make your final changes to the chart, Excel adds them to the chart picture displayed in the dialog box. When the chart picture in the dialog box looks the way you want, select OK. Excel then draws the chart and positions, or embeds, it in the worksheet location you specified. Figure 1-12 shows the South American bauxite production data in an area chart. The chart includes chart and axis titles and a legend.

15. **(Optional)** If the chart that Excel creates is the wrong size—too big or too small—click on the chart so that Excel adds selection handles, or white squares, to the four sides and four corners of the chart. Resize the chart area by

Figure 1-12: An area chart.

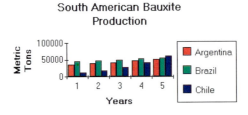

dragging the selection handles. Dragging a selection handle away from the chart increases the chart's and chart area's size; dragging a selection handle toward the chart decreases the chart's and chart area's size.

Using the Toolbar

As soon as Excel embeds a chart into a worksheet, it also adds a second toolbar, called the Charting Toolbar, to the Excel application window. Excel displays the Charting Toolbar any time an embedded chart is selected. Table 1-1 summarizes what the various charting tools do. The first 17 tools change the format of the selected chart. The eighteenth tool, Preferred Chart, changes the format of the selected chart to the default, or preferred, chart type. The nineteenth tool, ChartWizard, starts the ChartWizard so you can change the embedded chart. The last four charting tools, Horizontal Gridlines, Legend, Arrow, and Text Box, customize the embedded chart by adding gridlines, legends, arrows, and text to the embedded chart. Refer to Chapters 2 and 3 for examples and discussions of the different Excel chart formats. Refer to Chapter 5 for information on adding gridlines, legends, arrows, and text boxes to charts.

Table 1-1: The Charting Toolbar Tools.

Tool	Description
Area Chart	Changes the format of the selected chart to the first area-chart format
Bar Chart	Changes the format of the selected chart to the first bar-chart format
Column Chart	Changes the format of the selected chart to the first column-chart format

Table 1-1: The Charting Toolbar Tools. (Continued)

Tool	Description
Stack Column Chart	Changes the format of the selected chart to the third column chart format
Line Chart	Changes the format of the selected chart to the first line-chart format
Pie Chart	Changes the format of the selected chart to the sixth pie-chart format
XY Chart	Changes the format of the selected chart to the first xy-chart format
3D Area Chart	Changes the format of the selected chart to the fifth 3D area-chart format
3D Bar Chart	Changes the format of the selected chart to the first 3D bar-chart format
3D Column Chart	Changes the format of the selected chart to the first 3D column-chart format
3D Perspective Column Chart	Changes the format of the selected chart to the fifth 3D column-chart format
3D Line Chart	Changes the format of the selected chart to the first 3D line-chart format
3D Pie Chart	Changes the format of the selected chart to the sixth 3D pie-chart format
3D Surface Chart	Changes the format of the selected chart to the first 3D surface-chart format
Radar Chart	Changes the format of the selected chart to the first radar-chart format
Line/Column Chart	Changes the format of the selected chart to the first combination-chart format

Table 1-1: The Charting Toolbar Tools. (Continued)

Tool	Description
Volume/Hi-Lo-Close Chart	Changes the format of the selected chart to the fifth combination-chart format
Preferred Chart	Changes the format of the selected chart to the preferred-chart format
Chart Wizard	Starts the ChartWizard so you modify the selected chart.
Horizontal Gridlines	Adds horizontal gridlines to the selected chart.
Legend	Adds and removes a legend to/from the selected chart.
Arrow	Adds an arrow to the selected chart.
Text Box	Adds a text box to the selected chart.

Chart Design Fundamentals

The coming chapters delve more deeply into chart design fundamentals. Nevertheless, you should be familiar with a fundamental chart-design issue from the very beginning: which chart types make which data comparisons. Fortunately, this knowledge isn't difficult to acquire.

In a nutshell, there are actually only five types of data comparisons you can make with a chart, which means that selecting a chart type is dependent on the type of data comparison you want to make. Suppose, for the sake of illustration, that you were researching religion in the United States and had collected a large set of data. Assuming you had all the necessary data, there would be five data comparisons you could make:

- *Part-to-Whole Item Comparisons.* In a part-to-whole item comparison, you use a chart to show graphically what parts of some item make up the whole of the item. For example, if you want to show how the population of the United States of America breaks down by religious affiliation, you are making a part-to-whole comparison. The whole is the total U.S. population. The parts are the population segments that make up the whole: the part of the population that is Anglican, the part of the population that is Baptist, the part of the population that is Catholic, and so on.

- *Whole-to-Whole Item Comparisons.* In a whole-to-whole item comparison, you compare whole items to each other. You could use a whole-to-whole comparison, for example, to compare the absolute numbers of persons claiming religious affiliation (Anglicans, Baptists, Catholics, and so forth) with those claiming no religious affiliation (presumably agnostics and atheists).

- *Time-Series.* In a time-series comparison, you show how a variable changes (or doesn't change) over time. You would use a time-series comparison, for example, to show growth in the number of Anglicans in the United States over the last 10 years.

- *Correlation.* In a correlation comparison, you show or explore the relationship between two variables. You would use a correlation comparison, for example, to explore whether the national unemployment rate has an impact on the percentage of the population regularly attending a church or synagogue.

- *Data-Maps.* In a data-map chart, you use a geographic map to explore whether there's a relationship between a data series and geography. If you want to see whether there are really more Southern Baptists in the South, for example, you could use a map of the United States that colors states according to the percentage of Southern Baptists in the state.

Once you understand that there are only five basic data comparisons that can be made, it's usually easy to pick the appropriate Excel chart type. The different Excel chart types support different types of comparisons. In other words, the data comparison you want to make largely determines which chart type you should select.

Table 1-2 summarizes the five data comparisons, and details which Excel chart types support which data comparisons.

Excel's ability to create a data map is extremely limited. You are limited to mapping a rectangular area using a 3D surface chart. And you can't create a grid that corresponds to geographic boundaries.

As Table 1-2 indicates, in the case of correlation and data-map data comparisons, the type of comparison completely determines the appropriate Excel chart type. In the case of a part-to-whole comparison, you just choose between a regular pie chart and a 3D pie chart. For more information on picking a

Table 1-2: Data Comparisons and Chart Types

Comparison	Excel Chart Types
Part-to-Whole Item	Pie chart, 3D Pie chart
Whole-to-Whole Item	Bar, column, radar, 3D bar, 3D column, 3D surface
Time-Series	Area chart, column chart, combination chart, line chart, 3D area, 3D column, 3D line
Correlation	XY scatter chart
Data-Maps	3D surface

chart for whole-to-whole and time-series comparisons, refer to the next two chapters. They provide detailed discussions of each chart type's strengths and weaknesses—information that should help you select an appropriate chart type.

Printing and Saving Charts

You now know the steps for creating any Excel chart type using the ChartWizard. You've also learned about the types of data comparisons a chart makes and about how you pick the right Excel chart. There are, however, two other tasks with which you'll want to be familiar: how to print and how to save charts. The steps for accomplishing either task, though, depend on whether the chart is embedded in a worksheet or is, instead, stored and displayed in a separate chart document.

Printing and Saving Embedded Charts

Embedded charts are charts that sit, or float, on top of an Excel worksheet. If you followed the preceding section's steps for using the ChartWizard, for example, you created an embedded chart.

Embedded charts are actually pieces, or parts, of the Excel worksheet into which they're embedded. Because of this, if you print the area of the Excel worksheet in which the chart is embedded, you also print the chart. And, if you save the worksheet in which the chart is embedded, you also save the chart. Printing and saving embedded charts is, at least on the face of it, that simple.

I won't describe how you go about printing and saving Excel worksheets here. Presumably, you already know how to accomplish both of these tasks. If you don't know how to print or save Excel worksheets, you need to refer to the Excel user guide's discussion of the File Save As and File Print commands.

Printing and Saving Chart Documents

As mentioned earlier, charts don't have to be embedded in worksheets. You can display and store charts in their own, separate document windows. And, in fact, displaying and storing charts in separate document windows has some noteworthy advantages. Charts that are displayed and stored in separate document windows can be more easily and completely customized—something I'll describe in detail in Chapter 5, *Customizing Charts.* What's more, charts that are displayed and stored in separate document windows can be printed and saved separately from the underlying worksheet from which they get their data.

Document windows is a Microsoft Windows term. It refers to the windows that an application like Microsoft Excel displays in its application window. If you aren't familiar with the term and find its use confusing here, refer to the first chapter of the Windows user's guide.

The usual way to display and store a chart in its own separate document window is to just create in a separate document window in the first place. I'll describe how to do this in coming chapters. You can also copy an embedded chart to a separate document window. To do this, simply double-click on the embedded chart. Excel opens a new document window that displays a second copy of the chart. If you click on the embedded chart shown in Figure 1-12, for example, Excel opens a new document window with the same chart, as shown in Figure 1-13.

When the active document window shows a chart, Excel displays a new Charting menu bar, as shown in Figure 1-13. I'm not going to describe the Charting menu bar here, however, as

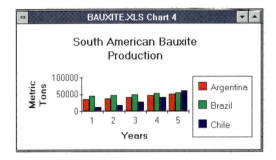

Figure 1-13: A chart document window.

the menu bar's menus and commands are described in the coming chapters. If you have a question about a specific tool or menu command, just refer to the index. It will give you the page number on which a particular command or option is described and illustrated.

Printing a Chart Document

To print a chart displayed in a separate document window, first make sure the chart's document window is the active one. You can tell whether a document window is active because its title bar will be dark. The title bars of inactive document windows are white. Once you're sure the chart's document window is active, activate the File menu and choose the Print command. Excel displays the Print dialog box, shown in Figure 1-14. To accept the default settings for printing a chart—and these will usually be fine—simply select OK.

To control the print quality, activate the Print Quality drop-down list box. The drop-down list box will show the alternative print resolutions in dots-per-inch, or DPI; you just select the one you want. The print quality trade-off is partly one of speed for quality. Lower DPI settings print more quickly, but they don't look as crisp on the page—especially in the case of charts. Higher DPI settings look better but they take longer to print. Higher DPI settings, however, also deliver two other important benefits in the case of chart printing: they make it

Figure 1-14: The print dialog box. If you want to fine-tune the chart-printing settings, you can specify print quality, the number of copies, and whether Excel should display the Print Preview window.

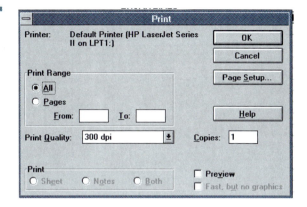

possible for you to chart larger numbers of data points because the chart detail is finer. Higher DPI settings also mean it's less likely your chart will show coarse, gritty grays and blacks, which tend to produce a moiré effect. For all of these reasons, you'll almost invariably want to use your printer's highest DPI setting.

A moiré effect is an optical illusion. It occurs when your eye tremors as it attempts to focus on a contrasting black and white spots, lines, or cross-hatching. As a result, the contrasting chart pattern—spots, lines, or cross-hatching, or whatever—appears to vibrate, or shimmer. A moiré effect can, and usually does, destroy a chart's readability.

To print more copies than one, move the selection cursor to the Copies text box. Then, type whatever number of copies you want.

To see how the printed chart will look on the page, mark the Print Preview Check box before you select OK. Then, when you select OK, Excel displays the Print Preview window with an example of how the printed chart will look on the page (see Figure 1-15).

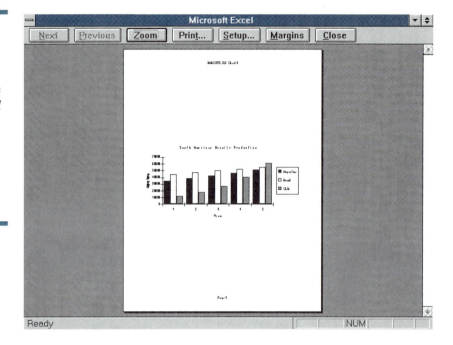

The Print Preview command butons are self explanatory, nevertheless, let's briefly review the function of each command button. Zoom alternately magnifies and reduces the chart page displayed on the Print Preview window. Because the details of a chart usually aren't legible when the entire chart page is displayed in the Print Preview window, you can use Zoom to review the details of a chart before printing the chart.

Print, just as you would expect, prints the chart displayed in the Print Preview window.

Setup displays the Page Setup dialog box, which (just as for regular worksheet printing) lets you change things like the page orientation, margins, paper size, headers, footers, and print dithering and intensity. For charts, the Page Setup dialog box also lets you specify the chart size using the Chart Size radio buttons: Size on Screen, Scale to Fit Page, and Use Full

Page. Mark the Size On Screen button if you want the printed chart to be the same size as it appears on the screen. Mark the Scale To Fit Page button if you want Excel to use normal scaling for the chart. ("Normal" scaling simply means the chart's width is slightly greater than its height—33 percent greater, to be exact.) Use Full Page expands the chart size so it fills the page.

Tip!

If at all possible, stay with the Scale To Fit Page, or normal charting scaling, option. Using a horizontal orientation, which is what results when you print using so-called normal scaling, is desirable for several reasons. It's been the traditional orientation of data graphics for at least a couple hundred years. It corresponds to a natural metaphor, the horizon, so people are used to and familiar with it. It provides for easier annotation and labeling and meshes more neatly with the Western tradition of reading from left to right. Finally, it tends to better emphasize cause-and-effect relationships in the data, particularly in the case of correlation graphics.

Margins displays lines on the chart page to show where the page margins are. You can change any of the chart page margins by dragging the margin lines toward or away from the page edge.

Close, of course, closes the Print Preview window. Use this command button when you don't want to print the chart and don't want to change any of the chart page settings.

Saving Chart Documents

Saving a chart document works the same way as saving a regular Excel worksheet. To save a chart document for the first time or to save a previously saved chart document using a new name, use the Save As command on the File menu. When you choose this command, Excel displays the Save As dialog box (see Figure 1-16).

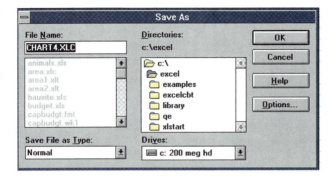

Figure 1-16: The Save As dialog box.

To complete the Save As dialog box, follow these steps:

1. Move the selection cursor to the File Name text box. Replace the default file name—the letters "Chart" followed by a number—with something more descriptive. You don't need to include the chart document file extension XLC. Excel will add it for you.

2. **(Optional)** If the drive shown in the Drives list box isn't the one on which you want to save the notebook file, move the selection cursor to the Drives list box, and select the drive on which the file should be stored.

3. **(Optional)** To store the file in a directory other than one that is listed, identify the directory by moving the selection cursor to the Directories list box, selecting the root directory, then selecting each of the directories in the path. (If you're not clear about how root directories, directories, and sub-directories are organized, refer to the *DOS User's Guide.*)

4. **(Optional)** To automatically create backup copies of the chart document file, assign a password to the saved chart document, or to display a message that recommends that someone open the chart document file as a read-only file, select the Options command button. Excel displays the

Save Options dialog box, which works for charts the same way it works for worksheets.

You can skip steps 2, 3, and 4 if you know the drive and directory of the stored file and the file extension for the desired format. Move the selection cursor to the File Name text box; then enter the complete path, file name and extension. Then, select OK. For example, if the current directory is C:\WINDOWS and you want to store the file named BAUXITE in the directory C:\EXCEL, enter C:\EXCEL\BAUXITE in the File Name text box. (As noted earlier, you don't need to enter the file extension, XLC because Excel adds it for you.)

5. When the Save As dialog box is complete, select OK to save the chart document as a file on your hard disk.

To save a chart document after it has already been saved once, select the Save command on the File menu. Because you've already given the chart document a file name and specified where it should be saved, Excel doesn't prompt you for additional information. It simply saves the chart document using the same name and directory.

Opening Previously Saved Chart Documents

Once you've saved a chart document as a file to disk, you can retrieve it from the disk anytime you want to use it or work with it again. To do this, you use the File menu's Open command.

1. Choose the Open command from the File menu. Excel displays the Open dialog box (see Figure 1-17).

2. **(Optional)** If the drive shown in the Drives list box isn't the one on which the file you want to retrieve is stored, move the selection cursor to the Drives list box and select the drive on which the file is stored.

Figure 1-17: The Open dialog box.

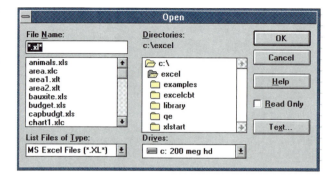

Tip!

As with the Save As command, you can skip steps 2 and 3 if you know the drive, directory, and extension of the stored file. Move the selection cursor to the File Name text box; then enter the complete path, file name, and extension. Then, select OK.

3. **(Optional)** If you want to retrieve a file from a directory other than one that is listed, identify the directory by moving the selection cursor to the Directories list box, selecting the root directory then selecting each of the directories in the path. (If you're not clear about how root directories, directories, and subdirectories are organized, refer to the *DOS User's Guide*.)

4. Move the selection cursor to the File Name text box. Enter the name of the chart document file you want to retrieve and the chart file extension, XLC. Or, select the chart document file from the list.

5. Select OK to retrieve the file from your hard disk.

6. Because a chart uses data from a worksheet file, Excel will ask you if you want to open the worksheet to which the chart is linked, by displaying a message box that asks, "Update references to unopened documents?" Select Yes if you want to open the worksheet to which the chart is linked; select No if you don't. (If you want to view or change the data graphed in the chart, be sure to select Yes.)

Using the Chart Templates On Disk

If you don't want to go to the work of creating your charts with the ChartWizard, you can use one of the chart templates on the disk that accompanies this book. By using the chart templates, you can create charts without having to know anything about Excel other than how to enter data into the worksheet and how to use the File Open command just described.

To use chart templates, you enter the worksheet data you want to chart, like the data shown earlier in Figure 1-1. Your data series and data categories should be easily interpreted by Excel—which simply means that your data series should each have more data points than the chart has data series. Next, you select the worksheet range that holds the data series names, category names, and data points. Then, you activate the File menu and choose the Open command so Excel displays the Open dialog box, as shown in Figure 1-17. As a final step, you enter the path, template file name, and the extension XLT in the File Name text box. For example, to use the template named AREA1.XLT with templates on the floppy disk in drive A, enter A:\AREA1.XLT. When you select OK, Excel opens a new chart document window and in it draws a chart using the chart template and the selected worksheet data. If you choose to create an area chart using Excel's first area chart format, the chart would look like that shown in Figure 1-18.

Chart templates are named using the type name (or what I hope is an easy-to-interpret abbreviation) and format number. So, the chart template AREA1.XLT is the chart template for an area chart, using the first area-chart format. And the chart template BAR2.XLT is the chart template for a bar chart, using the second bar-chart format.

For the names of the chart templates, refer to tables that accompany the discussions in Chapters 2 and 3 of each Excel

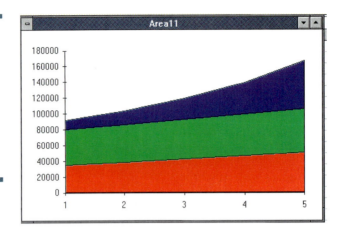

Figure 1-18: An area chart created using a template. The chart templates correspond to the predefined formats Excel provides.

chart type. For example, to learn the names of the two-dimensional area-chart templates, refer to Table 2-1 in Chapter 2.

The accompanying disk also includes chart templates formatted to work as 35mm chart slides. The 35mm-slide chart templates use a black background instead of a white background. In general, anything that would normally be black—like the chart text and axes—is instead white. (In a handful of cases, I've used gray in place of white because white was too bright.) Slide chart-template names give the chart type and format number and end with the letter S. So, the slide template AREA1S.XLT is the slide template for an area chart, using the first area-chart format. BAR2S.XLT is the slide template for a bar chart using the second bar-chart format.

Tip!

By the way, because the Excel color palette uses only a half dozen bright colors, you'll find the slide chart templates work best with data sets that include six data series or less. This shouldn't cause you problems because with slides you'll usually want fewer than six data series. When you want more than six data series, however, you'll want to customize a slide chart template so the coloring used for the seventh and any subsequent data series shows up on the black chart background.

Conclusion

This chapter covers an eclectic batch of topics in an attempt to make you quickly proficient in the mechanics of working with charts and in the fundamentals of good chart design. Where you go next really depends on what you want to do with Excel's powerful graphics features. If you're looking to become an expert, you may as well continue reading with the next two chapters, which describe how you go about working with the basic Excel chart types. If you're not looking to become an Excel charting expert, you can skip around, reading just those chapters that interest you or pertain to the charting task or tasks on which you're currently working.

2

Simple Charts

This chapter expands your charting knowledge by covering two important topics. It first describes how you go about creating charts without the ChartWizard so you can more quickly or flexibly create charts. Next, it delves more deeply into Excel's charting by describing the strengths and weaknesses of each of the simple Excel chart types: area charts, bar charts, column charts, line charts, and pie charts. The chapter also provides type-specific design ideas related to these charts.

Chapter 3 covers the strengths, weaknesses, and primary design issues related to the remaining Excel chart types: radar charts, xy (scatter) charts, combination charts, and each of the three-dimensional chart types.

Creating a Chart
Without the ChartWizard

You can choose to cook something from scratch or use pre-mixed ingredients. You can mix up the ingredients for a cake, for example, combining such things as flour, eggs, sugar, and so forth. Or you can use something like a Betty Crocker cake mix. The mix is easier, no doubt, but by working from scratch, you get to control exactly what ingredients go into your cake.

The same situation is true with Excel charts. As discussed in Chapter 1, you can create any Excel chart using Excel's ChartWizard. While this approach is certainly the easiest, it isn't as flexible as creating a chart from scratch.

Suppose, for the sake of illustration, you want to create an area chart. To create an area chart from scratch, follow the steps below, after you've constructed the worksheet that holds the data you want to plot.

1. Select the worksheet range that includes the data you want to plot, the series names, and the category names. To plot the data in Figure 2-1, for example, you would select the area A1:F4 because the range B1:F1 contains the category names, the range A2:A4 contains the series names, and the range B2:F4 contains the actual data.

2. Activate the Edit menu and choose the Copy command.

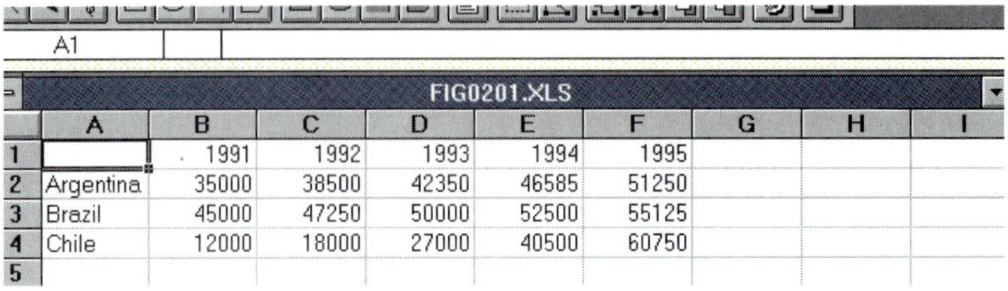

Figure 2-1:
Fictitious data
to chart.

	A	B	C	D	E	F	G	H	I
1		1991	1992	1993	1994	1995			
2	Argentina	35000	38500	42350	46585	51250			
3	Brazil	45000	47250	50000	52500	55125			
4	Chile	12000	18000	27000	40500	60750			
5									

3. Open a chart document window by choosing the New command from the File menu and selecting the Chart option from the list box that Excel displays, as shown in Figure 2-2.

4. Activate the Edit menu and choose the Paste Special command. Excel displays the Paste Special dialog box, as shown in Figure 2-3.

5. Use the Values (Y) In radio buttons to indicate whether the data-series values are stored in rows or in columns. In Figure 2-1, for example, the data-series values are stored in rows, so you would mark the rows radio button.

As mentioned in Chapter 1, Excel assumes that your chart data will always have more categories than series. In the case of the South American bauxite production, for example, Excel assumes that the data series are in rows because, when you exclude series and category names, there are three rows and five columns of chart data.

Figure 2-2: The New dialog box.

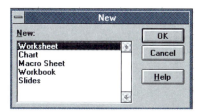

Figure 2-3: The Paste Special dialog box.

6. If data-series values are arranged by row and data-series names are stored in the first column of a chart data range, mark the Series Names In First Column check box. (Or, if data-series values are arranged by column and data-series names are stored in the first row of a chart data range, mark the Series Names In First Row check box.)

If it contains text, Excel assumes that the first column in a data-series-by-row worksheet selection and the first row in a data-series-by-column worksheet selection stores the data-series names. Because cells A2, A3, and A4 hold text, for example, Excel assumes that column A in Figure 2-1 contains data-series names.

7. If data-series values are arranged by row, and category names are stored in the first row of the chart data range, mark the Categories (X Labels) in the First Row check box. [(Or, if data-series values are arranged by column, and category names are stored in the first column of the chart data range, mark the Categories (X Labels) in the First Column check box.)]

Excel assumes that the first row in a data-series-by-row selection or the first column in a data-series-by-column selection contains category names if the first cell in the row or column is blank. Because cell A1 is blank, for example, Excel assumes that row 1 in Figure 2-1 contains category names.

8. When the Paste Special dialog box correctly describes the chart data range, select OK. Excel pastes the chart data into the empty chart document window using the preferred, or default, chart type and format. If you haven't changed the preferred, or default, chart type and format, Excel draws the new chart as the first column chart for-

mat. (Chapter 5, *Customizing Your Excel Charts*, describes how you change the preferred chart type.)

Tip!

If Excel can correctly interpret the series and categories in the chart data range because your chart data includes more categories than series, you can skips steps 2 through 8. In their place, you can press the shortcut —F11—for opening a new chart document window. Excel then opens a chart document window and draw the preferred chart type and format in the window.

9. To change the initially displayed chart type, activate the Gallery menu and choose the chart type you want (see Figure 2-4). To create an area chart, for example, choose the Area command; Excel displays the area chart version of the Chart Gallery dialog box, as shown in Figure 2-5. If you select another chart type from the Gallery menu, of course, Excel displays the version of the Chart Gallery dialog box that shows valid formats for the chart type.

The Previous and Next command buttons move you backward and forward through the different versions of the Chart Gallery dialog box. Excel arranges the different versions in the

Figure 2-4: The Gallery menu. Activate the Gallery Menu to choose a chart type.

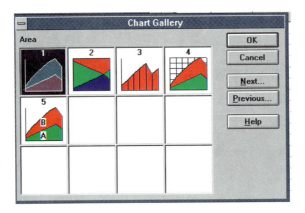

Figure 2-5: The Chart Gallery dialog box. This dialog box shows valid formats for the chart type you choose.

same order they appear on the Gallery menu. So, if you display the area chart version of the dialog box, then select the Next command button, the bar chart version of the dialog box will appear.

10. Select one of the chart formats by clicking on the format or by highlighting the format with the navigation keys; then select OK or press Enter. Excel changes the type and format of the chart in the document window to whatever you select. Figure 2-6 shows an example area chart.

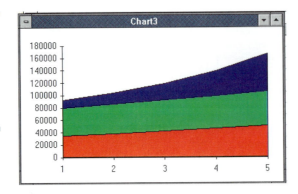

Figure 2-6: An area chart. The area between lines shows the relative size of each data series.

Area Charts

An area chart, like the one shown in Figure 2-6, plots data points using lines, and then it stacks the lines so they show cumulative values. The area between lines, which is colored or shaded, shows the size of each data series relative to the total of all the data series. In Figure 2-6, for example, the first area shows Argentina's bauxite production. The second area shows Brazil's. The third area shows Chile's.

Excel, by default, uses the category names—which in this case are the years—to label the horizontal axis, which crosses the vertical axis at zero. Excel scales the value axis so it calibrates both the smallest and largest data markers. Generally, this results in the value axis scale ranging from either 0 (or if plot negative values to slightly less than the smallest data point value) to slightly more than the largest data-point value.

Area Chart Format Descriptions

Excel provides five area chart formats. Table 2-1 on the following page summarizes the five area chart formats and identifies the names of the regular chart templates and the 35mm-slide chart templates from the disk that you can use to create area charts in each of the five formats. (Refer to Chapter 1 if you want to use a template but don't know how.)

Area Chart Format 1: A Simple Area Chart

The first area chart format, which I'll label a simple area chart, shows overall trends in the first data series and in the total of all the data series. For example, the area chart in Figure 2-6 shows the general trend in Argentinean bauxite production and the general trend in total South American production. Note, however, that the area chart in Figure 2-6 doesn't show—or doesn't clearly show—the general trends in the second and subsequent data series because the lines plotting the

Description	Format	Regular Template	Slide Template
Simple area chart	1	AREA1.XLT	AREA1S.XLT
Area chart with 100% scaling of the Y-axis scale	2	AREA2.XLT	AREA2S.XLT
Area chart with drop lines	3	AREA3.XLT	AREA3S.XLT
Area chart with horizontal and vertical gridlines	4	AREA4.XLT	AREA4S.XLT
Area chart with data-labeled areas	5	AREA5.XLT	AREA5S.XLT

Tip!

The first four area chart formats don't identify the data series. If you need identification, you'll want to add a legend when using these formats. You can add a legend using the Charting Toolbar's Legend tool.

second and subsequent data series are actually cumulative. The second line plots the total of the first and second data points. The third line plots the total of the first, second, and third data points.

Area Chart Format 2: A 100 Percent Area Chart
The second area chart format is an area chart with 100 percent scaling of the value axis. It shows each data series' data-point values as a percentage of the total data series' data-point values. Because of the 100 percent scaling, you can more easily compare the relative sizes of the plotted data series to the total data series. Figure 2-7 shows the same data as Figure 2-6, but this time uses the 100 percent area chart. The 100 percent area charts are useful for showing percentage-share information over time. For example, if you want to show how the market percentage shares of South American bauxite producers have changed over time, you can use a 100 percent area chart.

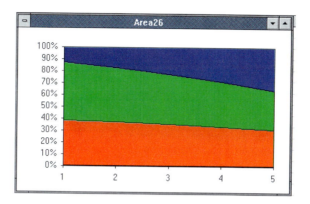

Figure 2-7: The second area chart format. A 100% area chart is useful for showing percent-age-share information over time.

Area Chart Format 3: An Area Chart with Drop Lines

The third area chart format adds vertical drop lines, which identify the data points to the simple area chart format, as shown in Figure 2-8. Area charts with drop lines show not only overall trends in the first data series and for the total data series, they also show the number of data points. You can verify this statement by comparing Figure 2-6, which has no drop lines, with Figure 2-8, which has drop lines.

Area Chart Format 4: An Area Chart with Gridlines

The fourth area chart format closely resembles the first, except that it also uses vertical and horizontal gridlines, as shown in

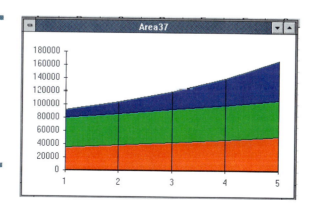

Figure 2-8: The third area chart format. The drop lines in this chart show data series trends and the number of data points.

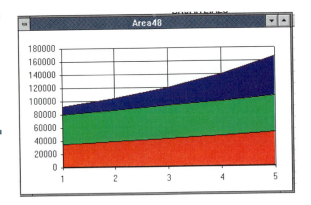

Figure 2-9: The fourth area chart format. This area chart uses vertical and horizontal gridlines.

Figure 2-9. Excel draws horizontal gridlines at the major vertical-axis increments, or *tick marks*, and it draws vertical gridlines at the major horizontal-axis increments. In theory, gridlines make it easier to compare data-point values: your eye can, for example, follow a gridline to the adjoining axis. Note, however, that unless you use an area chart format with drop lines, you won't know what the actual data points are. Because this format doesn't provide drop lines, it doesn't really make sense to add the gridlines.

Area Chart Format 5: An Area Chart with Data Labels

The fifth area chart format places data series names in the different series' areas, as shown in Figure 2-10. Figure 2-10 illus-

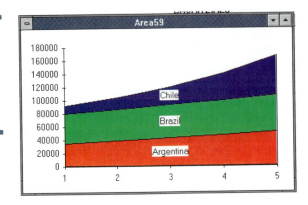

Figure 2-10: The fifth area chart format. Data labels directly identify data series.

trates a potential problem with the other four area chart formats: in the absence of a legend, people viewing the area chart won't necessarily know the identity of the plotted data series.

In general, data labels are superior to chart legends for a simple reason. With data labels, you learn the identity of a plotted data series when you look at it. Legends, in comparison, require you to look back and forth between the chart's plot area and the legend. For this reason, whenever you create area charts that plot more than a single data series, you'll probably want to use this area chart format.

Area Chart Strengths

Area charts possess several strengths. They allow you to legibly plot many more data points than you would be able to with some chart types because data points are simply points on a line. Even with the relatively low resolutions available on output devices like printers, for example, you can still legibly plot hundreds of data points using an area chart.

Area charts work well for showing trends in the first data series and in the total of the plotted data series. Note, however, that you can't use area charts for showing trends in any individual data series but the first because the lines that plot the second and subsequent data series are actually cumulative.

Finally, area charts, because they stack the lines that create the areas, work well when adding two or more data series together to create a third implicit data series. For example, businesses calculate profits using the formula *revenue - expenses = profits*. Or, you can restate this profit formula *revenue = profits + expenses*. So, by plotting two data series, one for profits and one for expenses, in an area chart you implicitly show a revenue data series data as well. Figure 2-11 shows an example of this technique.

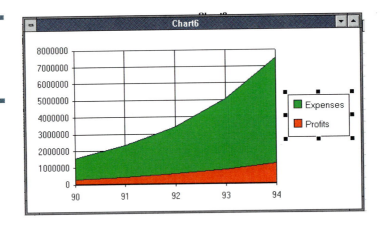

Figure 2-11: An area chart with an implicit data series.

Area Chart Weaknesses

Area graphs suffer several deficiencies, however. The lines and between-line areas tend to visually overpower the data-point values, so comparing data points is extremely difficult. Without drop lines, in fact, it becomes very difficult to know how many data points there are and what the actual data-point values are. In the case of the first data-series points, you actually only know they fall somewhere on the line. And data-point comparisons of the second and any subsequent series are next to impossible because Excel plots the *cumulative* totals.

Area graphs may suggest trends that do not exist. It has been said many times before, but let me repeat an important truth: A time-series graph, which is what an area chart is, suggests that time itself is a variable. In the case of the South American bauxite production, the area chart suggests that the progression of time itself has in some way caused the increase in bauxite production. The chart also suggests that as time continues—that is, as we move into the future—the production increases will continue. Of course, this is nonsense. Almost certainly, there are other independent variables that do a much better job of explaining the change in the data-point values and, therefore, any trends in the data.

Area charts possess yet another weakness. While you can look at the first data-series area and see trends in the data-point values, you can't do the same for the second and subsequent data-point values. These areas are actually cumulative and even though the line and area for the second data series rises, the data-point values for this second series may be falling.

Area Chart Design Issues

Perhaps the most important design issue related to area charts is the organization of the underlying chart data in the worksheet. In general, you'll want the data series that is the most important to visually calibrate to be the first series. It is, after all, the only one you'll be able to easily measure against the value axis.

Data organization is also important when you're creating 100 percent area charts. Notice, for instance, how the area chart in Figure 2-12 supports the message used as the chart's title—that Brazilian bauxite production has eroded the market shares of Argentina and Chile. Notice, too, how the area chart in Figure 2-13 supports the message used as that chart's title—that Brazil's production increases have come at the expense of Argentina. (This may be obvious to you, but I should point out that Figures 2-12 and 2-13 use data different from that shown in Figure 2-1.)

There's a point that's important to make regarding Figures 2-12 and 2-13. While you can visually inspect the charts and easily deduce the messages about the growth in Brazil's percentage share, the striking appearance of the chart may exaggerate the significance of, or even misrepresent, the data's message. The actual data used in Figure 2-12 had Brazil's production increasing at a rate much faster than that of Argentina and

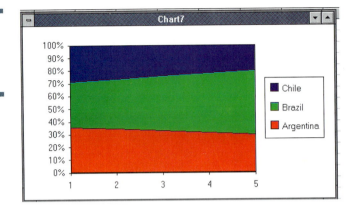

Figure 2-12:
*Brazil is gaining
a larger market
share.*

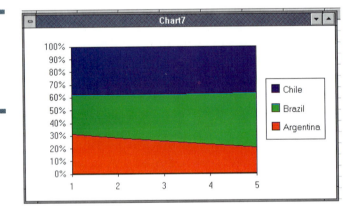

Figure 2-13:
*Brazil's
increases come
at the expense of
Argentina.*

Chile. And the actual data used in Figure 2-13 had Argentina's production flat, Chile's production growing at 10 percent, and Brazil's production growing at 20 percent. (By the way, when you want to compare rates of growth, you need to use logarithmic value scaling. Refer to Chapter 5, *Customizing Your Charts*, for details on how to do this.)

There are several minor design issues you'll want to consider as you create and work with area charts. These are all pretty obvious, so I'll just list them in quick fashion. You don't need to identify the data series twice, so if you use the fifth area chart format, which supplies data series names as labels, don't use a legend. You can't use the area chart with drop lines if you're plotting large data sets because the drop lines become over powering. You should usually avoid the area chart format with gridlines; the gridlines can't be used to calibrate data-point values you can't see.

Bar Charts

Bar graphs work well for graphing single or multiple data series. They are particularly useful when you want to compare the values in a single data series in something other than a time-series analysis. The reason is that each data point is plotted using a separate horizontal bar. Figure 2-14 shows more fictitious South American mining data in dollars. Figure 2-15 shows the mining data in a bar chart.

As Figure 2-15 shows, Excel uses the category names—gold, silver, copper, iron, and lead—to label the vertical axis, which then becomes the category, or x, axis. Excel then uses the horizontal axis as the values, or y, axis. As with other chart types, Excel sets the minimum and maximum values that appear on the y-axis scale by reading the plotted data. Typically, it sets the minimum value to either 0 or slightly less than the smallest data point and the maximum value to slightly more than the largest data point.

Figure 2-14: More fictitious South American mining data.

	A	B	C	D	E	F	G	H	I
		Gold	Silver	Copper	Iron	Lead			
1									
2	Argentina	35000	38500	42350	46585	51250			
3	Brazil	45000	47250	50000	52500	55125			
4	Chile	12000	18000	27000	40500	2500			
5									
6									

MINING.XLS

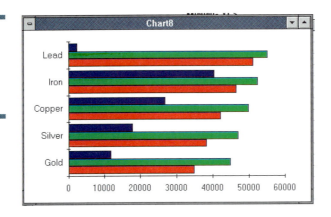

Figure 2-15: A bar chart, using fictitious South American mining data.

Bar Chart Format Descriptions

Excel provides 10 bar chart formats. Table 2-2 summarizes the 10 bar chart formats and identifies the names of the regular and the 35mm-slide chart templates from the disk, which you can use to create bar charts in each of the formats.

Table 2-2: Bar Chart template descriptions and names.

Description	Format	Regular Template	Slide Template
Simple bar chart	1	BAR1.XLT	BAR1S.XLT
Bar chart for single data series	2	BAR2.XLT	BAR2S.XLT
Stacked bar chart	3	BAR3.XLT	BAR3S.XLT
Bar chart with overlapped bars	4	BAR4.XLT	BAR4S.XLT
Stacked bar chart with 100% scaling of Y-axis	5	BAR5.XLT	BAR5S.XLT
Bar chart with vertical gridlines	6	BAR6.XLT	BAR6S.XLT

Table 2-2: Bar Chart template descriptions and names (Continued).

Description	Format	Regular Template	Slide Template
Bar chart with vertical gridlines	6	BAR6.XLT	BAR6S.XLT
Bar chart with data-labeled bars	7	BAR7.XLT	BAR7S.XLT
Bar chart with no spacing between bars	8	BAR8.XLT	BAR8S.XLT
Stacked bar chart with lines connecting bars in the same data series	9	BAR9.XLT	BAR9S.XLT
Stacked bar chart with 100% scaling of Y-axis and lines in the same data series connecting bars	10	BAR10.XLT	BAR10S.XLT

Tip!

None of the bar chart formats identify the plotted data series. If identification is required, you'll need to add a legend, which you can do by using the Legend tool on the Charting Toolbar.

Bar Chart Format 1: A Simple Bar Chart

The first bar chart format, which I'll label a simple bar chart, uses different colored horizontal bars for each data series. It also arranges together the first data-point set, or category, of each of the series for comparison; the second data-point set, or category, of each of the series for comparison, and so on. In the bar chart you saw back in Figure 2-15, for example, Excel shows Argentina's mining production in red, Brazil's in green, and Chile's in blue. The bars that show how much gold each country produced appear together. Similarly, the bars that show how much silver, copper, iron, and lead by each country produced also appear together.

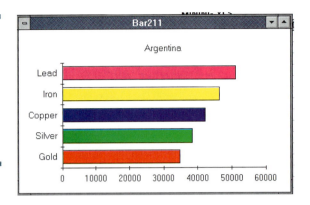

Bar Chart Format 2: A Bar Chart for a Single Data Series

The second bar chart format is used when you want to plot a single data series. Figure 2-16 shows an example of the second bar chart format, showing the amount of gold, silver, copper, iron, and lead produced by a single country, Argentina. Excel uses different colors for each bar. If you include the data series name in your worksheet selection, Excel uses the name as the chart title.

Bar Chart Format 3: A Stacked Bar Chart

The third bar chart format, the stacked bar chart, simply stacks the bars that make up the graph, as shown in Figure 2-17. You use stacked bar graphs when data points whose bars get stacked add up to a meaningful total and you want see how a

Figure 2-17: The third bar chart format. The stacked bar graph allows for data-point comparisons against the total.

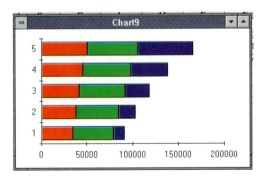

data-point value relates to the total. For situations where you have only a handful of data points, stacked bar graphs make it easy to compare data-point totals and see how each data series relates to the total. In the case of the South American bauxite production, for example, stacking the bars gives you both the visual indication of the total South American bauxite production and the relative production share of each country.

Bar Chart Format 4: A Bar Chart with Overlapping Bars
The fourth bar chart format is just like the first bar chart format except that bars overlap in a category (as shown in Figure 2-18). The first data series' bars overlap the second data series' bar, the second data series' bar overlaps the third data series' bars, and so on. Overlapping the bars does a couple of things: it lets you show more data on a bar chart because you've got room for a greater number of bars, and it more closely ties together the bars in a category, such as the gold-mining production bars, the silver-mining production bars, the copper-mining production bars, and so forth.

Bar Chart Format 5: A 100 Percent Stacked Bar Chart
The fifth bar chart format is a 100 percent stacked bar chart. It shows each data series' data-point values as a percentage of

Figure 2-18: The fourth bar chart format. The overlapping bar chart allows for more bars and the grouping of bars in a category.

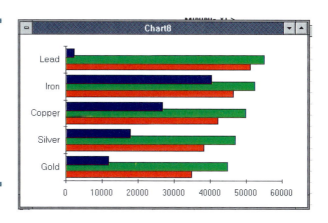

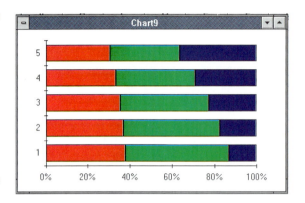

the total data series' data-point values, thereby allowing comparison of the relative sizes of the plotted data series to the total data series. Figure 2-19 shows the same data as Figure 2-17, except this time it uses the 100 percent stacked bar chart. To show the relative percentages of bauxite mined by various South American countries, you can use a 100 percent stacked bar chart.

Bar Chart Format 6: A Bar Chart with Vertical Gridlines

The sixth bar chart format adds vertical gridlines to the simple bar chart format. These gridlines should make it easier for you to compare data-point values. Your eye can, for example, follow one of the vertical gridlines to the horizontal, or value, axis. Figure 2-20 shows a bar chart with vertical gridlines.

Bar Chart Format 7: A Bar Chart with Value Labels

The seventh bar chart format places the actual data-point values at the end of the bars that plot the values (see Figure 2-21). While this information can be very helpful, you shouldn't use this format unless you later plan to customize the chart graph either by removing the horizontal axis or, at the very least, by removing the values that calibrate the horizontal axis. It's redundant to have both the value axis and the value labels—

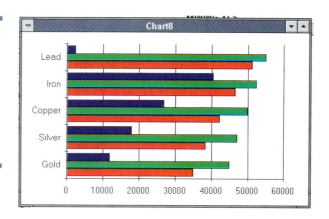

Figure 2-20: The sixth bar chart format. Excel draws vertical gridlines at the major horizontal-axis increments.

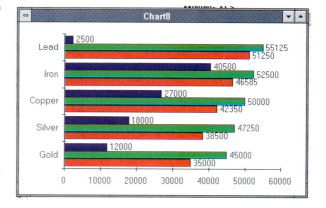

Figure 2-21: The seventh bar chart format. This bar chart places the data-point values at the end of the bars that plot values.

it's also messy. (For information on how to modify a value axis, refer to Chapter 5, *Customizing Your Charts*.)

Excel displays values in the labels the same way they are formatted on the worksheet from where they come.

Bar Chart Format 8: A Bar
Chart with No Spaces Between Bars

The eighth bar chart format closely resembles the first bar chart format. The only difference is that for the eighth format Excel doesn't leave any spaces between the different catego-

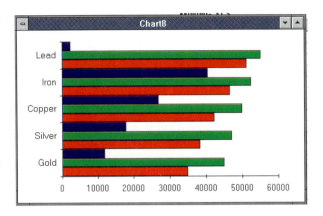

Figure 2-22: The eighth bar chart format. This bar chart allows you to include more data points in the chart by eliminating space.

ries, as shown in Figure 2-22. You use this format to pack more bars and, therefore, more data points onto a bar chart. You won't be able to distinguish one bar from another easily, however. Nor will you as easily be able to distinguish between categories. For these reasons, you'll probably want to avoid using this bar chart format except when you're plotting a single series with a large number of data points.

Bar Chart Format 9: A Stacked Bar Chart with Lines Connecting Bars

The ninth bar chart format is just a stacked bar with lines drawn between the bars, as shown in Figure 2-23. Compare Figure 2-23, a stacked bar chart with lines connecting the bars, to Figure 2-17, a stacked bar chart without lines connecting the bars. Like the regular stacked bar chart, you use stacked bar charts with connecting lines when data points with stacked bars add up to a meaningful total, and you want see how a particular data-point value relates to the total.

Bar Chart Format 10: A 100 Percent Stacked Bar Chart with Lines Connecting Bars

The tenth bar chart format is a 100 percent stacked bar chart with lines drawn between the bars, as shown in Figure 2-24.

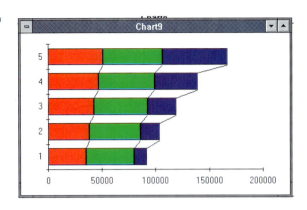

Figure 2-23: The ninth bar chart format. This format makes it easier for your eyes to follow each data series because the connecting lines let you move easily between categories.

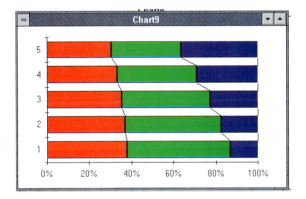

Figure 2-24: The tenth bar chart format. This stack bar chart format shows lines between bars.

Like the regular 100 percent stacked bar chart (see Figure 2-19), this bar chart format shows each data-series' data point values as a percentage of the total data series' data-point values, thereby allowing comparison of the relative sizes of the individual data series. As with the format described in the preceding paragraph, the lines that connect the bars of data series may make it easier for your eye to move between the bars of a data series.

Bar Chart Strengths

Bar charts are extremely useful for making whole-item to whole-item data comparisons when the categories aren't time periods. Each data point is represented by a single data marker—a bar. It's easy to identify, calibrate, and compare the data-point values. Because the value axis isn't horizontal, there isn't any confusion about the chart showing time-series data. Finally, the horizontal chart's orientation allows for lengthier, more legible category names.

Bar Chart Weaknesses

There are weaknesses associated with bar charts, however. The first weakness stems from the fact that each data point is depicted in a separate bar. Excel allocates space on the vertical, or categories axis, based on the number of data points. This means that the greater the number of data points, the more narrow your bars. Even with a relatively small amount of data, then, your bar charts can quickly become cluttered with too many bars and almost illegible because of the skinny width of the bars. A bar chart of five data series with 10 data points each, for example, results in a 50-bar chart.

The stacked bar chart formats possess a weakness also inherent in area charts. You can easily calibrate the data markers of the first data series, but you can't do the same thing for the second and subsequent data series because these data series markers are stacked on top of the preceding data series.

Bar Chart Design Issues

The main design issue for bar charts concerns the organization of the data you want to plot. While there's the inevitable temptation—probably a carryover from grade school—to arrange data series or categories in alphabetical order, there's usually another order that makes more sense given the chart message. For example, if your message is that a certain breakfast food is very low in the grams of fat per serving size, you might want to arrange the bars in the order of data-point values rather than alphabetically by category name. Figures 2-25 and 2-26

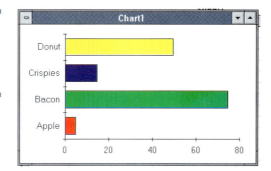

*Figure 2-25:
Alphabetic
arrangement
of bars.*

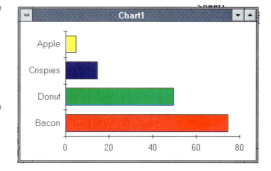

*Figure 2-26:
Ascending-
data-points
arrangement
of bars.*

depict the same data, a single series showing fat content of popular breakfast foods. Figure 2-25 shows the data points arranged in alphabetical order by category name. Figure 2-26 shows the data points arranged in data point value order. Doesn't the data point value ordering scheme better support the chart message? I think so.

There are also a couple of minor design issues that I'll mention in passing. First, when you work with the bar chart that has overlapping bars, you should (usually) place the smallest data series first, the next-smallest data series second, and so forth, so legibility isn't obscured. Just as you pose people by height when you take a group photograph, it's easier to see all the bars on a bar chart if the short bars are in front and the tall bars are in back. (This organizational scheme becomes more important the larger the number of data points you plot, because as the number decreases, a smaller and smaller slice of the overlapped bars shows.)

A second design issue for bar charts concerns category names. As noted in the discussion of bar chart strengths, you have room for much larger category names on a bar chart. In most cases, then, you'll want to take advantage of this bar chart strength to make your charts easier for people to understand, by using lengthier, more descriptive category names rather than cryptic abbreviations or codes. Category abbreviations like "Mkg," "Mfg," and "Mgt," for example, should be replaced with the complete category names "Marketing," Man-ufacturing,"and "Management."

Column Charts

Column charts work well for plotting time-series data because the horizontal category axis can be used to show the progres-sion of time. On column charts, each data point is plotted using a separate vertical bar. Typically, bars representing one data series are the same color, but are differentiated from the bars of other data series that are shown in other colors. Figure 2-27 again shows the fictitious South American bauxite mining data. Figure 2-28 shows the mining data in a column chart. The red bars show Argentina's bauxite production. The green bars show Brazil's production. The blue bars show Chile's.

The reason a column chart works so well for time-series data is that people are used to looking at charts that use the hori-zontal axis to show time. This particular charting convention has, in fact, been used for slightly more than 200 years.

Excel, by default, uses the category names—which in this case are the year numbers—to label the horizontal axis. As for bar charts, Excel scales the value axis by looking at your data. In

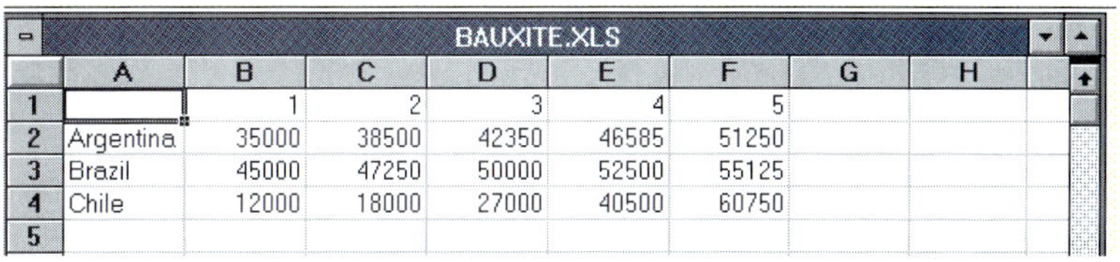

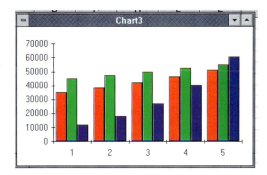

Figure 2-27: The fictitious South American baux- ite data.

Figure 2-28: A column chart.

general, Excel scales the value-axis minimum to either 0 or, if you plot negative values, to slightly less than the smallest value; and it scales the value-axis maximum value slightly more than the largest data point.

Column Chart Format Descriptions

Excel provides 10 column chart formats. Table 2-3 on the following page summarizes the 10 column chart formats and identifies the names of the regular and the 35mm-slide chart templates from the disk that you can use to create column charts in each of the 10 formats.

As a careful comparison of Tables 2-2 and 2-3 indicates, Excel's bar chart and column chart formats are essentially identical. The only difference is in their orientation. In a bar chart, the bars and value axis are horizontal, while the category axis is vertical. In a column chart, the columns and value axis are vertical, while the category axis is horizontal.

Table 2-3:
Column Chart
Template
Descriptions
and Names.

Description	Format	Regular Template	Slide Template
Simple column chart	1	COL1.XLT	COL1S.XLT
Column chart for single data series	2	COL2.XLT	COL2S.XLT
Stacked column chart	3	COL3.XLT	COL3S.XLT
Column chart with overlapped columns	4	COL4.XLT	COL4S.XLT
Stacked column chart with 100% scaling of Y-axis	5	COL5.XLT	COL5S.XLT
Column chart with horizontal gridlines	6	COL6.XLT	COL6S.XLT
Column chart with data-labeled columns	7	COL7.XLT	COL7S.XLT
Column chart with no spacing between columns	8	COL8.XLT	COL8S.XLT
Stacked column chart with lines connecting columns in the same data series	9	COL9.XLT	COL9S.XLT
Stacked column chart with 100% scaling of Y-axis and lines connecting columns in the same data series	10	COL10.XLT	COL10S.XLT

None of the column chart formats identify the data series. If identification is needed, add a legend using the Charting Toolbar's Legend tool.

Column Chart Format 1: A Simple Column Chart

The first column chart format, which I'll label a simple column chart, uses different colored vertical columns for each data series. It also arranges the first data point set, or category, of each of the series together for comparison, the second data point set, or category, of each of the series together for comparison, and so on. In the column chart in Figure 2-28, for example, Excel shows Argentina's mining production in red, Brazil's in green, and Chile's in blue. The columns that show how much bauxite each country produced for year 1 appear together. So do the bars for year 2, year 3, and so forth.

Column Chart Format 2:
A Column Chart for a Single Data Series

The second column chart format is used when you want to plot a single series. Figure 2-29 gives an example of the second column chart format, showing the annual bauxite production for a 5-year period for Argentina. With a single-series column chart, Excel uses a different color for each column: red for the first data point's column, green for the second, blue for the third,

Figure 2-29: The second column chart format. A single-series column chart uses a different color for each column.

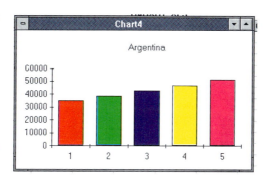

and so on. If you include the data series name in the worksheet range selection, Excel uses the name as the chart title.

Column Chart Format 3: A Stacked Column Chart

The third column chart format is a stacked column chart. This
column chart format just stacks the columns that make up the
chart, as shown in Figure 2-30. You use stacked column charts
when data points, whose columns get stacked, add up to a
meaningful total, and you want see how a data point value
relates to the total. For situations where you have only a handful of data points, stacked column charts make it easy to compare category totals and show how each of the data-series
values relates to the total. With the South American bauxite
production data, for example, stacking the columns gives you
both a quick visual indication of the total South American
bauxite production and a more detailed look at each country's
production as a percentage of the total production.

**Column Chart Format 4: A
Column Chart with Overlapping Columns**

The fourth column chart format is just like the first format except
that columns overlap in a category, as shown in Figure 2-31. The
first data series' columns overlap the second data series' columns, the third data series' columns-overlap the third data
series' columns, and so on. Overlapping the columns does two

*Figure 2-30: The
third column
chart format.
The stacked col-
umn chart lets
you see how a
data-point value
is related to the
total.*

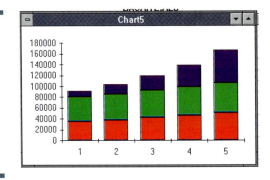

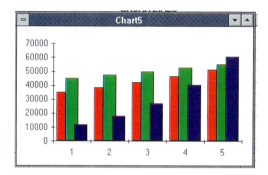

Figure 2-31: The fourth column chart format.

things: it lets you show more data because you've got room on the category axis for columns, and it lets you more closely tie together the bars in a category, such as the bauxite production for year 1.

Column Chart Format 5:
A 100 Percent Stacked Column Chart

The fifth column chart format is a 100 percent stacked column chart. It shows each data series' data-point values as a percentage of the total data series' data-point values, thereby comparing the relative sizes of the plotted data series to the total data series. Figure 2-32 shows the same data as Figure 2-30, except that this time the figure uses a 100 percent stacked column chart. If you wanted to show how the production percentage shares of South American bauxite producers had changed over

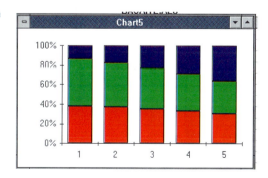

Figure 2-32: The fifth column chart format. 100% stacked column charts, like 100% area charts, show percentage-share information over short periods.

time, you could use a 100 percent stacked column chart. Note, though, that with larger numbers of data points, a 100 percent area chart usually works just as well.

Column Chart Format 6:
A Column Chart with Horizontal Gridlines

The sixth column chart format just adds horizontal gridlines to the simple column chart format, as shown in Figure 2-33. The perhaps obvious purpose of these gridlines is to make it easier for you to compare data-point values. In effect, they make it easier to calibrate columns that aren't next to the value axis.

Column Chart Format 7:
A Column Chart with Value Labels

The seventh column chart format places the actual data-point values at the end of the bars that plot the values, as shown in Figure 2-34. Adding value labels to the columns makes it possible for people to precisely know data-point values. For this reason, if you do choose to use this column chart format, you'll want to consider removing the value axis, because it's redundant to have both the value axis and the value labels. (For information on how to modify a value axis, refer to Chapter 5, *Customizing Your Charts.*)

Figure 2-33: The sixth column chart format. Excel draws horizontal gridlines at the major value-axis increments.

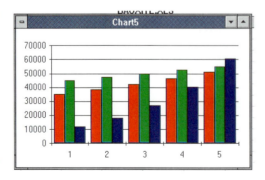

Figure 2-34: The seventh column chart format. Value labels draw the reviewer's eye to specific data-point values.

Excel displays values in the labels the same way they are formatted on the worksheet from where they come.

Column Chart Format 8: A Column Chart with No Spaces Between Columns

The eighth column chart format differs from the first column chart format in just one way. In the eighth column chart format, Excel doesn't leave any spaces between the different categories columns. Figure 2-35 shows an example of a column chart with no spaces between the columns. As is the case with its bar chart cousin, you can use the "no-spaces-between-bars" column chart to pack more bars and, therefore, more data onto a chart, but you won't be able to easily distinguish between categories. Because of this, you would usually choose this col-

Figure 2-35: The eighth column chart format.

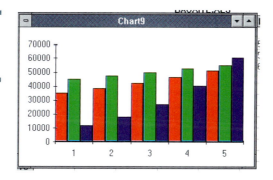

umn chart format when you're plotting only a single series with a large number of data points, and you don't want to use another column chart format because it would result in narrow, illegible bars.

**Column Chart Format 9: A Stacked
Column Chart with Lines Connecting Columns**

The ninth column chart format is just a stacked column chart with lines drawn between the columns, as shown in Figure 2-36. Like the other stacked column chart format, you use this format when the categories you're plotting add up to a meaningful total. As noted in the earlier discussion of the other stacked column chart format, area charts also let you accomplish many of the same things.

**Column Chart Format 10: A 100 Percent
Stacked Column Chart with Lines Connecting Columns**

The tenth and final column chart format is a 100 percent stacked column chart with lines drawn between the columns, as shown in Figure 2-37. Like the other 100 percent stacked column chart (see Figure 2-32), this column chart format shows data point values as a percentage of all the data-points

*Figure 2-36: The
ninth column
chart format.
The connecting
lines of this
column chart
format make it
easier for you to
visually follow
the bars of each
data series.*

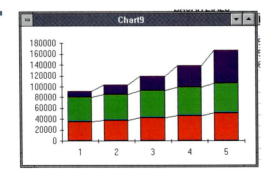

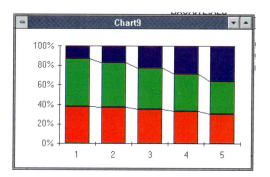

Figure 2-37: The tenth column chart format. With the connecting lines, this format may make it easier for the eye to move between the columns of a data series.

in the category, making it easier to compare the relative sizes of the data points in your series.

Column Chart Strengths

Column charts work extremely well for making whole-item to whole-item data comparisons when the categories are time periods. Each data point is represented by a single data marker—a column so it's easy to identify, calibrate, and compare the data-point values.

Another strength relates to the orientation of the chart type. With the horizontal categories axis, column chart categories can be easily used to show the passage of time. In fact, because people are used to seeing time-series data depicted with a horizontal axis, you probably wouldn't want to plot non-time-series data with a column chart.

Column Chart Weaknesses

Predictably, however, column charts are not without their weaknesses. First of all, Excel allocates space for the bars on the horizontal categories axis based on the number of data points. The greater the number of data points, of course, the narrower the bars. So, even with a relatively small amount of data, your column chart quickly becomes cluttered and even worse, sometimes illegible.

Because there's less room for category names under the category axis, it's usually harder to clearly identify categories in column charts as, compared to, say, bar charts. In a 12-month time series, for example, you won't have room to neatly fit the full month names—January, February, March, and so on. You may be able to get around this space limitation by changing the typeface point size or the orientation of the category names. Both of these techniques are described in Chapter 5, *Customizing Your Charts*.

As is the case with other time-series charts, of course, column charts may suggest trends that do not exist. A time-series graph, such as a column chart, suggests that time itself is a variable. Almost certainly, however, there are other independent variables that do a much better job of explaining the change in the data-point values and, therefore, any trends in the data.

Finally, the stacked column chart format possesses another weakness. While you can easily calibrate the columns of the first data series because they abut against the category axis, you can't do the same for the second and subsequent data-point values. The reason, of course, is that these subsequent data-series columns abut against the preceding data-series columns and not the category axis.

Column Chart Design Issues

The structure of the column chart format suggests several design conventions. First of all, you'll probably want to use column charts solely for time-series plots. People are used to seeing a horizontal category axis showing the passage of time. What's more, the Excel bar chart has advantages over the column chart when you're plotting non-time-series data.

Another thing to consider is this: when you work with a column chart that has overlapping bars, you should usually place the smallest data series first, the next-smallest data series second, and so forth. This way, the shorter bars appear in the front of the taller bars, and you can still easily gauge each bar's equivalent data-point value. This sort of data organization becomes more important the larger the number of data points you plot, because a smaller and smaller slice of the overlapped bars shows.

One other thing you'll want to think about when you work with column charts is your category names. This is because you have so little space. In general, you'll want to use as short a category name as people can easily understand. So, rather than 1992, you might use 92. Rather than June 1992, you might use 6/92. Or if the year isn't important, you might use just 6. Excel uses the same formatting as the cells containing your category names. You can use worksheet formatting to control the numeric format of the dates used to identify categories.

Finally, remember that when your data series include a great many data points, a column chart becomes visually similar to an area chart. Hence, when you're working with column charts that contain a great many data points, you'll usually want to consider the same issues as you do for area charts. Rather than repeat myself here, however, I'll just refer you to the earlier discussion of area chart design issues.

Line Charts

Line charts work well when you've got a large data set to plot, and particularly when your data series include many data points. Line charts may also be useful for showing time-series trends and for highlighting simple relationships between the plotted data series.

For a line chart, Excel plots data points as symbols and then draws lines between each data series' data points. To differentiate the data series, Excel uses either different data-point symbols or different colored lines. Figure 2-38 shows sample data such as you might plot in a line chart: sales revenue for two competitive companies, Mammoth and Acorn. Figure 2-39 shows the sales revenue and advertising expenditures plotted in a line chart. The line with the red data-marker symbols shows Acorn's revenue. The line with the green data-marker symbols shows Mammoth's revenue.

Tip!

Figure 2-39 uses columns to store the data series rather than rows. For charts with large data sets, you'll often want to follow this column-oriented data organization. Remember that Excel allows for 255 data series and 4,000 data points in a series. To reach these limits, however, you need to store your data series in columns since the Excel worksheet provides 256 columns.

Figure 2-38: Sample sales data.

	A	B	C	D	E	F	G	H
1	Year	Acorn	Mammoth					
2	1	1,000,000	10,000,000					
3	2	1,500,000	10,500,000					
4	3	2,250,000	11,025,000					
5	4	3,375,000	11,576,250					
6	5	5,062,500	12,155,063					
7								

Figure 2-39: A line chart.

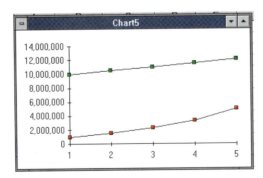

Excel uses the category names—which in this case are the year numbers—to label the horizontal axis. Typically, Excel scales the value axis from a minimum value of either 0 or, if you plot negative values, slightly less than the smallest value, to a maximum value that is slightly larger than the largest data point.

Line Chart Format Descriptions

Excel provides nine predefined line chart formats, as documented in Table 2-4. Note that Table 2-4 also gives the regular and 35mm-slide template names, in case you want to create one of these line charts by using a template from the disk. The basic differences in the formats relate to the data markers used to show the data points and the type of scaling used for the value axis.

Table 2-4: Line Chart Template Descriptions and Names

Description	Format	Regular Template	Slide Template
Line chart with both line and symbol data markers	1	LINE1.XLT	LINE1S.XLT
Line chart with just line data markers	2	LINE2.XLT	LINE2S.XLT
Line chart with just symbol data markers	3	LINE3.XLT	LINE3S.XLT
Line chart with both line and symbol data markers, plus horizontal gridlines	4	LINE4.XLT	LINE4S.XLT
Line chart with both line and symbol data markers, plus horizontal and vertical gridlines	5	LINE5.XLT	LINE5S.XLT

Description	Format	Regular Template	Slide Template
Line chart with logarithmic scale	6	LINE6.XLT	LINE6S.XLT
Line chart with high-low data markers	7	LINE7.XLT	LINE7S.XLT
Line chart with high-low-close data markers	8	LINE8.XLT	LINE8S.XLT
Line chart with open-high-low-close data markers	9	LINE9.XLT	LINE9S.XLT

Tip!

None of the line chart formats identify the data series. If identification is required, you'll want to add a legend. The easiest way to add a legend is using the Charting Toolbar's Legend tool.

Line Chart Format 1: A Line Chart with Both Line and Symbol Data Markers

The first line chart format shows both lines and symbol data markers for each of the plotted data series. Each data series is plotted with a separate line. To differentiate the data series, Excel uses different colored data-marker symbols—small squares in Figure 2-39—to show the data-point values. Because the data-marker symbols are large, you wouldn't usually use this line chart format when you want to plot data series with more than a hundred data points because the symbols start to overlap.

Line Chart Format 2: A Line Chart with Only Lines But No Symbol Data Markers

The second line format is just like the first except that it uses only lines and no symbol data markers. Figure 2-40 shows an example of the second line chart format. Because the second line chart format doesn't have different colored symbol data markers to differentiate each data series, Excel uses different

Figure 2-40: The second line chart format. Line charts that use only lines emphasize the changes between data points, and deemphasize individual data points.

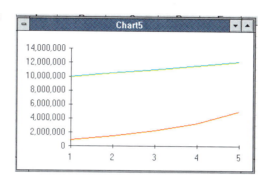

colored lines: red for the first data series line, green for the second data series line, and so on. (In fact, the only way you can identify specific data points on a lines-only line chart is when the line for a data series changes direction: in other words, data points occur between the short, straight-line segments.)

Line Chart Format 3: A Line Chart with Only Symbol Data Markers

The third line chart format is just the first line chart format with one difference. The third format uses no lines; it uses only symbol data markers (see Figure 2-41). Excel uses color to segregate data points into data series. With the standard Excel

Figure 2-41: The third line chart format. Line charts that use only symbol data markers emphasize individual data points and deemphasize changes between them.

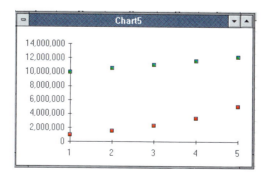

color palette, for example, Excel uses red for the first data series symbol data markers, green for the second, and so on.

Even with their relative emphasis of individual data-point values and their de-emphasis of the changes between data points, lineless line charts usually don't work well when you're plotting a large data set. Here's the reason: with any line chart, Excel doesn't allocate exclusive, horizontal chunks of the categories axis to each data point. For this reason, if the first and second data series' first data-point values are exactly the same, Excel plots the second data-series symbol data marker on top of the first data-series symbol marker, thereby hiding it. If this sounds confusing, consider the way that Excel plots bars and columns in bar and column charts. When Excel plots a bar or column chart, it positions the bars and columns either side by side or slightly overlapped. You can still view each data marker.

Line Chart Format 4: A Line Chart with
Line and Symbol Data Markers Horizontal Gridlines

The fourth line chart format adds horizontal gridlines to the first line chart format (see Figure 2-42 for an example). The horizontal gridlines make it possible to more precisely calibrate the changes in data-point values as well as individual data-point values.

Figure 2-42: The fourth line chart format.

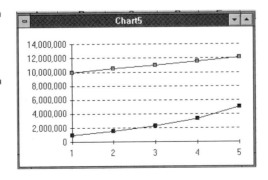

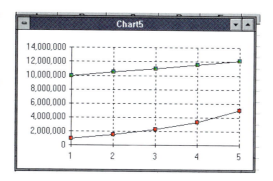

Line Chart Format 5: A Line Chart with Both Line and Symbol Data Markers, Plus Horizontal and Vertical Gridlines

The fifth line chart format adds both horizontal and vertical gridlines to the first line chart format. As noted in the preceding paragraph, the horizontal gridlines make it possible to more precisely calibrate the changes in data-point values as well as individual data-point values. The vertical gridlines make it easier to identify the categories. Figure 2-43 shows an example of this line chart format.

Line Chart Format 6: A Line Chart with Logarithmic Values Scale

Line charts with logarithmic scaling of the value axis, like the sixth line chart format, let you plot the rate of changes in data-point values rather than the actual changes in data-point values. To understand the powerful nature of logarithmic scaling, take another look at Figures 2-38 and 2-39, the make-believe sales data of two imaginary companies, Mammoth and Acorn. If you look at Figure 2-39, you can see that Mammoth is much larger than Acorn. In addition, it appears, at least after simple analysis, that the relative sizes of the two companies have remained almost the same over the time period for which the data is plotted. This isn't actually the case, however. I created

Figure 2-44: The sixth line chart format.

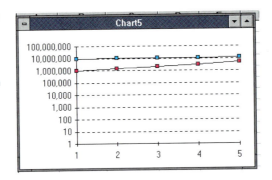

the fictitious sales data in Figure 2-38 by starting Mammoth's annual sales at $10,000,000, and then annually increasing this figure by 5 percent, and by starting Acorn's annual sales at $1,000,000, and then annually increasing this figure by 50 percent. Obviously, if Acorn continues its annual growth of 50 percent and Mammoth continues it's annual growth of 5 percent, Acorn sales are actually closing in on Mammoth's sales. In fact, if these two annual sales rates continue, Acorn will quite quickly grow to be larger than Mammoth. Yet this isn't apparent from the simple line chart shown in Figure 2-39. If you plot a line chart using logarithmic scaling, however, the fact that Acorn is growing much faster than Mammoth immediately becomes evident because with logarithmic scaling a line chart shows the rate of change (see Figure 2-44). Mammoth's line's data markers are green, by the way; Acorn's line's data markers are red.

Line Chart Format 7: A Line
Chart with High-Low Data Markers
The last three line chart formats are most frequently used for something called *technical security analysis*: the plotting of daily stock prices in an attempt to gain insight that lets a securities analyst better predict future stock-price changes. In the seventh line chart format, Excel plots two data series: the first data series is daily high prices for a stock, and the second data

Figure 2-45: The seventh line chart format.

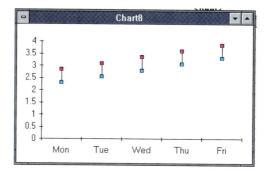

Figure 2-45: The seventh line chart format.

series is the daily low for stock, as shown in Figure 2-45. Notice that in a high-low line chart, Excel doesn't use lines to connect the data points of each data series, but to connect the data points of each category. Each day's stock price information represents a category.

Line Chart Format 8: A Line
Chart with High-Low-Close Data Markers

In the eighth line chart format, Excel plots three data series containing daily stock price information: the stock's high price, the stock's low price, and the stock's closing price. To show the stock's daily high and low prices, Excel draws a vertical line from the low price to the high price. To show the closing price, Excel draws a horizontal dash, which sticks out from the left side of the high-low line. Figure 2-46 shows the eighth line chart format.

Figure 2-46: The eighth line chart format.

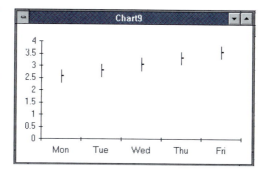

*Figure 2-47: The
ninth line chart
format.*

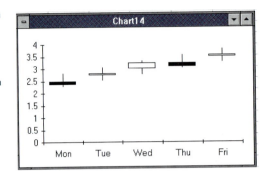

Line Chart Formats 9: A Line Chart
with Open-High-Low-Close Data Markers

In the ninth and final line chart format, Excel plots four data series containing daily stock-price information: the stocks opening price, the stock's high price, the stock's low price, and the stock's closing price. To show the stock's daily high and low prices, Excel again draws a vertical line from the low price to the high price. To show the opening and closing prices, Excel draws a box. The top and bottom sides show the opening and closing prices. If the box is white, the closing price exceeds the opening price. If the box is black, the opening price exceeds the closing price. Figure 2-47 shows the ninth line chart format.

Tip!

The three high-low line chart formats that Excel provides were originally created for securities analysis. While you can, of course, use them for graphical securities analysis, the three formats can be even more valuable for plotting other types of data. In fact, any time you're plotting two, three, or four data series that are closely related—daily temperature information, for example—it may be more useful to visually link with a line the data points in a category rather than the data points in a series.

Line Chart Strengths

Line charts let you plot very large data sets, as long as you don't use symbol data markers. In fact, line charts represent one of the only chart types you can use to plot the largest data set possible in Excel—a data set with 255 data series and 4,000 data points per data series. (Your other two possible options for plotting monstrously large data sets are the area chart type and the 3D area chart type. Both work well when you have a large number of data points but not a large number of data series.)

What's more, line charts—more than any other Excel chart format—emphasize changes in the data points rather than the data points themselves. This lets you more easily compare things like the absolute changes in data-point values using regular, arithmetic scaling. And, you can more easily compare the rates of change in data-point values using logarithmic scaling.

The high-low line chart formats also possess a third strength. They let you closely tie together, by a connecting line, the data points in a category.

Line Chart Weaknesses

Not surprisingly, of course, line charts also possess a few weaknesses. As noted in more than one of the line chart format descriptions, the data markers on a line chart can easily obscure one another. For this reason, line charts shouldn't (usually) be used when you want chart viewers to compare data point values.

Another problem with line charts is that, like every other time-series graph, they may suggest time-based trends that don't, in fact, exist. As I've noted in earlier discussions, time is rarely the best independent variable for explaining why a data series' data points change.

Line charts may also suggest relationships between data series that don't exist. For example, two lines rising together may suggest some correlation that doesn't actually exist. Two lines oscillating together may even more strongly suggest some correlation that doesn't actually exist.

The reverse can also be true because of the way Excel scales the value axis: two data series that actually are related won't always appear to be related. For example, the monthly interest income earned on a $1,000,000 cash account would depend entirely on the interest rate paid that month. However, if you plot interest rates—which might be running from 3 percent to 9 percent (or, stated as decimal values, from .03 to .09)—and the resulting monthly interest income—which would run from $2,500 to $7,500 a month—Excel scales the value axis so it starts as zero and stops at around $8,000. In this case, the plotted interest-rate line looks flat—as though it's equal to zero. Figure 2-48 shows an example of this problem. Notice that the red interest-rate line actually lies right on top of the category axis.

To show the relationship between two data series like interest rates and monthly interest income, you would need to use either an xy chart or a combination chart. Both of these chart formats are described in the next chapter.

Figure 2-48: A line chart with a problem.

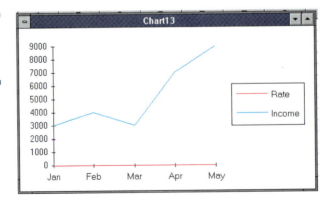

Line Chart Design Issues

The most important design issue related to line charts is probably adopting the convention that the chart type be used only for time-series graphs. This suggestion stems from the line chart type's horizontal category axis, of course. As mentioned earlier, people are used to seeing horizontal category axes showing the passage of time.

Another thing you'll want to think about when you work with line charts is the length of the category names. You don't have much space for category names. In general, you'll want to use as short a category name as possible for people to easily understand. In place of 1992, for example, you might use 92. In place of June, you might use just 6. (Excel, as noted earlier, uses the same formatting for category names as the worksheet cells containing category names. So use worksheet formatting to control the numeric format of the dates used to identify categories.)

Let me just bring up again a couple of design issues raised in the discussions of the various line chart formats. Because line charts don't segregate the data points in each category very well, don't use a format with symbol data markers if you're working with large data sets. As I pointed out early in this chapter section on line charts, Excel will often overwrite the data markers of another series when you're using the line chart format.

What's more, *do* consider using the line chart format with logarithmic scaling when what you want to show is the rate of change in a data series. My experience is that while most people would never consider logarithms a useful tool for presenting data, it's usually easy to down play the fact that they have even been used. Instead, one can simply focus viewers' attention on what has actually been plotted: the rate of change.

Pie Charts

Pie charts show the relationship between individual data points and the total of all the data points in a single series. As you undoubtedly know, Excel draws a circle and then slices the circle into as many wedges as there are data-points in the plotted data series. The size of a wedge, of course, depends on the data-point value and the total of all the data point values in the series. Excel, for example, shows a data-point value that's 25 percent of the total as a wedge equal to a quarter of the circle.

To differentiate data points in the data series, Excel uses different colored wedges; can explode one or more wedges; and, optionally, labels wedges. Figure 2-49 shows sample data that you might plot in a pie chart: South Argentina's mineral production. Notice that pie charts plot only a single data series.

Figure 2-50 shows the data from Figure 2-49 plotted in a pie chart. The red wedge shows the first data-point value, the Argentinean bauxite production. The green wedge shows the Brazilian data-point value. The blue wedge shows the Chilean data-point value. Excel positions the first data point's wedge—the gold data point value in Figure 2-50—so it starts at the 12 o'clock position. Subsequent wedges follow in clockwise fashion. The second wedge abuts the first wedge. The third wedge abuts the second. The fourth abuts the third, and so on. If you provide a data series name, as I did in Figure 2-49, Excel uses it as a chart title.

Figure 2-49: Sample pie chart data.

	A	B	C	D	E	F	G	H	I
1		Argentina's Mineral Production							
2	Gold	35000							
3	Silver	38500							
4	Copper	42350							
5	Iron	46585							
6	Lead	51250							
7									

MINING.XLS

Figure 2-50: A
pie chart.

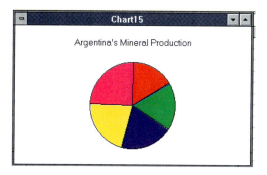

Pie Chart Format Descriptions

Excel provides seven predefined pie chart formats, as documented in Table 2-5. Note that Table 2-5 also gives the regular and 35mm slide template names in case you want to create one of these pie charts by using a template from the accompanying disk. The two basic differences among the formats relate to whether Excel labels the wedges of the pie chart and whether Excel explodes one or more of the wedges.

Table 2-5: Pie
Chart Template
Descriptions and
Names.

Description	Format	Regular Template	Slide Template
Simple pie chart	1	PIE1.XLT	PIE1S.XLT
Black-and-white pie chart with labeled slices	2	PIE2.XLT	PIE2S.XLT
Pie chart with first slice exploded	3	PIE3.XLT	PIE3S.XLT
Pie chart with all wedges exploded	4	PIE4.XLT	PIE4S.XLT

Table 2-5: Pie Chart Template Descriptions and Names (Continued).

Description	Format	Regular Template	Slide Template
Pie chart with category-labeled wedges	5	PIE5.XLT	PIE5S.XLT
Pie chart with percentage-labeled wedges	6	PIE6.XLT	PIE6S.XLT
Pie chart with both category- and percentage-labeled wedges	7	PIE7.XLT	PIE7S.XLT

Tip!

Many of the pie chart formats don't identify the categories. If you need this identification, add a legend using the Charting Toolbar's Legend tool.

Pie Chart Format 1: A Simple Pie Chart

The first pie chart format just shows the data-point values as different colored, proportional wedges, as shown in Figure 2-50. As long as you haven't modified the Excel colors palette or customized the pie chart, Excel colors the first pie slice red, the second pie slice green, the third pie slice blue, and so on, continuing with the remaining colors in the palette.

Pie Chart Format 2: Black-and-White Pie Chart with Labeled Slices

The second pie chart format plots the pie chart in black and white. It also uses the category names to identify the wedges. Figure 2-51 shows an example of this format. To make room in the chart area for the category names, Excel draws a smaller pie.

Pie Chart Format 3: A Pie Chart with First Slice Exploded

Figure 2-52 shows the third pie chart format, in which Excel simply explodes the first wedge of the pie. The exploded first-

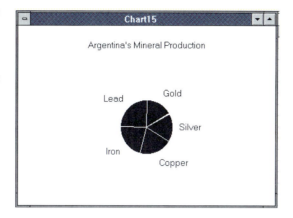

Figure 2-51: The second pie chart format.

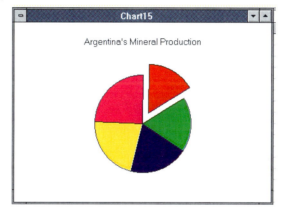

Figure 2-52: The third pie chart format.

pie chart wedge draws attention to the first wedge. Use this format if the first data-point value is small relative to the other data points plotted, but you need to retain emphasis of the first data point.

Pie Chart Format 4: A Pie Chart with All Wedges Exploded

The fourth pie chart format, shown in Figure 2-53, explodes all the wedges of the pie. You can successfully plot a few more data points in a pie chart when each of the wedges are

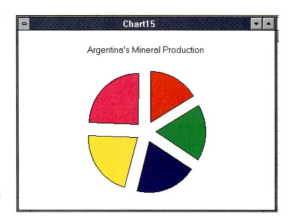

Figure 2-53: The fourth pie chart format. Because Excel explodes each of the wedges here, there's no added emphasis placed by the exploded wedges.

exploded. For example, many data analysts and graphic designers suggest that it's difficult to plot more than five or six data points in a pie chart because some of the wedges get too small to see. With every wedge exploded, however, you may be able to plot a few extra data points.

Pie Chart Format 5: A Pie Chart with Category-Labeled Wedges

Figure 2-54 shows the fifth pie chart format. To help viewers identify the plotted data, this format labels the wedges in a pie

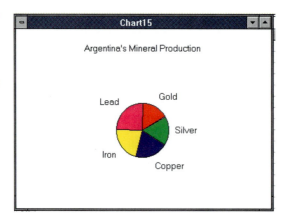

Figure 2-54: The fifth pie chart format.

with category names. In effect, the fifth pie chart format is simply the second format with color added.

As for the second format, to make room for the category name labels, Excel draws a smaller pie.

Pie Chart Format 6: A Pie Chart with Percentage-Labeled Wedges

The sixth pie chart format labels the wedges of the pie with percentages. Figure 2-55 shows an example of this. In a way, these percentage labels are redundant if you believe that pie charts successfully show the relative size of data-point values compared to the total of all the data-point values. I suppose you might decide to include these percentage labels, however, if you wanted to add precision to a particular pie chart.

Pie Chart Format 7: A Pie Chart with Both Category- and Percentage-Labeled Wedges

The last pie chart format is really just a combination of the fifth and sixth formats: This format, as shown in Figure 2-56, includes both category labels and percentage labels. To make room for the category labels, Excel draws a smaller pie. As noted in the preceding format description, the percentage

Figure 2-55: The sixth pie chart format.

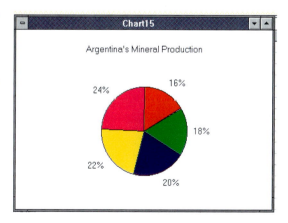

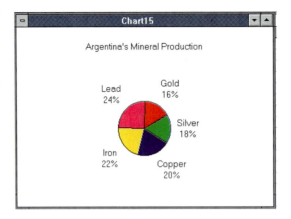

Figure 2-56: The seventh pie chart format.

labels are a little odd if you believe that pie charts successfully show relative data point values anyway.

Pie Chart Strengths

Quite frankly, a pie chart doesn't have many strengths. In fact, when you compare its merits to those of the usual alternatives, it may have none. Some people suggest that people's familiarity with this chart type is a strength. Others suggest that pie charts have value as a design gimmick. I don't buy either of these arguments, and I'll explain why in the next paragraph.

Pie Chart Weaknesses

Pie charts possess several weaknesses. Two are extremely serious. The first and biggest weakness is that they can't communicate more than a single data series nor more than a handful of data points. So, you can't use them to summarize large data sets. And, you can't use them to make comparisons between two or more data sets. In fact, if you look at the usual applications of pie charts, it's often the case that they are being used to cover up embarrassingly small data sets.

Another weakness is that by the time you add the necessary category and percentage labels, you can usually improve the power of the information you're communicating by getting rid of the pie wedges and building a table instead. If you create a table that shows category names and percentages, for example, it will do a much better job of communicating the information contained in Figure 2-56. A table would also open up several new communication opportunities. You could show actual data-point values, for example. And, if you wanted, you could include many more categories.

A third and final weakness of the pie chart type is that they aren't as easy to annotate. Any notes you use to describe pie chart wedges end up in an arc around the edges of the pie. Figures 2-54, 2-55, and 2-56, which include category and percentage labels, illustrate this visual problem. To read this information, your eyes must move clockwise around the edges of the pie.

Pie Chart Design Issues

If you choose to use a pie chart in spite of its weaknesses, there are several things you should do. First, be sure you don't plot more data points on the pie chart than are legible. How many is too many data points depends on your data set. And, as noted earlier, you may be able to fit more wedges into a pie chart by using the exploded format. If a viewer can't easily discern one or more wedges, however, you've plotted too many data points.

Second, if you want to emphasize a relatively small data point, make sure it's the first data point in the series. The reason for this is that Excel positions the first data point at the 12 o'clock position, and the 12 o'clock wedge position is usually the most visible part of the circle. If you want to show that a data point is very large, however, you usually don't need to worry about where its wedge is.

Third, don't use redundant category identifications by includ-ing both category labels and a category legend. As noted ear-lier, category labels are usually easier for a viewer to read, so they are preferable to category legends. (A legend is more work for a viewer's eyes because it requires the reader to look back and forth between the legend and the pie chart.)

Conclusion

You need to carefully choose the chart type and format you use to visually show a particular data set. Most—although not all—of the simple Excel chart types and formats have useful appli-cations. The trick is to pick a chart type that supports your message. In choosing a chart type, of course, you'll want to consider each chart type's strengths and weaknesses and their effect on the message or messages you want to communicate.

3

Advanced Charts

In addition to the chart types described in Chapter 2, Excel provides several additional chart types. I've chosen to call these additional types advanced charts because they use multiple value axes or three dimensions. These advanced chart types include radar charts, xy charts, combination charts, and each of the three-dimensional chart types. Some of the advanced charts—particularly the radar and xy chart types—greatly expand your opportunities for communicating and understanding data. Other chart types, quite frankly, are dangerous and inappropriate graphic tools which should never be used. In the pages that follow, I'll identify and describe the various chart types.

Radar Charts

Radar charts let you plot data points using a value axis for each category. If you haven't seen the chart type before, it can be a little confusing. Once you're familiar with the chart type, however, you will find radar charts are a powerful graphic tool because they let you precisely compare the relative sizes of each data series' data point. Figure 3-1, for example, shows the amount of sodium, fat, and sugar contained in three fictitious junk foods: Deep-fries, Salties, and Sweeties.

Excel uses a value axis for each category by arranging value axes around a central origin. Each data point is plotted directly on top of the appropriate value axis. Then, to identify which data points together make up a data series, Excel draws lines between data point markers.

The benefit of this chart type may seem small at first, but take a look at Figure 3-2. It shows the data from Figure 3-1 plotted in a radar chart. From the chart, it becomes clear that Deep-fries is the junkiest of the three junk foods. This visual insight, however, wouldn't be as apparent if you used, say, a bar chart, as shown in Figure 3-3.

As Figure 3-2 shows, if you include category names in the worksheet range you select for plotting, Excel uses those names to label the axes. If you include data-series names in the worksheet range you select for plotting, you can also add a legend using the series names.

Figure 3-1: Fictitious data for a radar chart.

	A	B	C	D	E	F	G
		Sodium (mg)	Fat (mg)	Sugar (mg)			
1							
2	Deep-fries	100	150	100			
3	Salties	50	75	45			
4	Sweeties	15	20	125			
5							

JUNKFOOD.XLS

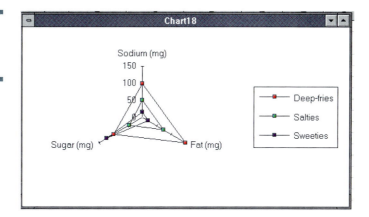

Figure 3-2: An example radar chart.

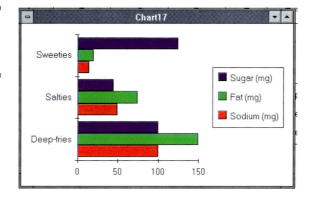

Figure 3-3: The equivalent bar chart.

So that Excel can draw lines between the data points, you also need at least three categories to make the chart type work.

Radar Chart Format Descriptions

Excel provides five radar chart types, as identified in Table 3-1. The basic differences between chart types involve what type of markers Excel uses to plot your data: lines, symbols, or both lines and symbols. Table 3-1 also names the chart templates from the disk, which you can use to quickly create any of these radar chart types.

Table 3-1: Radar Chart Template Descriptions and Names.

Tip!

None of the radar chart formats automatically provide a legend to identify data series. If you want a legend, you need to add it.

Description	Format	Regular Template	Slide Template
Radar chart with both line and symbol data markers, plus value axes	1	RADAR1.XLT	RADAR1S.XLT
Radar chart with line data markers, plus value axes	2	RADAR2.XLT	RADAR2S.XLT
Radar chart with just line data markers but no value axes	3	RADAR3.XLT	RADAR3S.XLT
Radar chart with line data markers, value axes, and gridlines	4	RADAR4.XLT	RADAR4S.XLT
Radar chart with logarithmic scale	5	RADAR5.XLT	RADAR5S.XLT

Radar Chart Format 1: A Radar Chart with Line and Symbol Data Markers, and Value Axes

The first radar chart format, which is shown in Figure 3-2, uses both symbol and line data markers. Excel uses different colors for the symbol data markers. It draws black lines to connect the symbols. Note that the symbol data markers aren't necessary for identifying data points, however. In a radar chart, the lines cross the value axes at data-point values.

Legends aren't automatically included in the first radar chart format. I added the one shown in Figure 3-2 to make it easier to explain the chart type.

In general, you use the first radar chart format when, as your primary objective, you want to focus attention on individual data-point values using the symbol data markers and, as your secondary objective, you want to visually connect with a line to identify a group of data points that belong together in a data series. For example, the data set shown in Figure 3-1 probably works best with the first radar chart format because while you want to focus attention on the actual sodium, fat, and sugar content of each snack food, you also want snack foods to be assessed by looking at all their combined elements—sodium, fat, and sugar.

Radar Chart Format 2: A Radar Chart with Only Lines

The second radar chart format, which is shown in Figure 3-4, is simply the first radar chart format minus the symbol data markers. The first data series, Deep-fries, is plotted in red. The second data series, Salties, is plotted in green. The third data series, Sweeties, is plotted in blue.

Figure 3-4: The second radar chart format. By removing the data markers, you deemphasize the actual values plotted and emphasize the data series plot-ted.

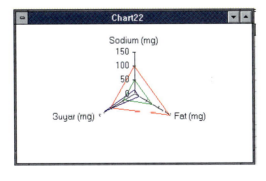

As noted earlier, you can still tell exactly where the data point values occur because the lines cross the value axes at the data point values. Accordingly, you lose no information by removing the symbol data markers. What you do lose, however, is visual emphasis. This deemphasis can be effective for certain types of chart messages. Figure 3-4, for example, might support such a message as "In two out of three categories, Salties is the junkiest junk food" and do it better than alternative graph types.

Radar Chart Format 3: A Radar Chart with Lines But No Value Axes

The third radar chart format is just like the second, except that it doesn't have the value scales, as shown in Figure 3-5. Without the value axes, of course, it becomes impossible to calibrate data-point values—which suggests you won't have many uses for this format.

Radar Chart Format 4: A Radar Chart with Line Data Markers, Value Scales, and Gridlines

The fourth radar chart format shows lines, value axes, and gridlines connecting the value axes, as shown in Figure 3-6. This is a curious chart format if you consider that fact that the purpose of a radar chart is to use different value axes for each

Figure 3-5: The third radar chart format. This format focuses attention on the relative magnitude of the different data series.

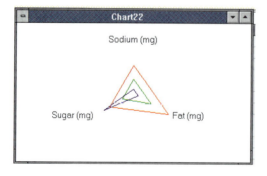

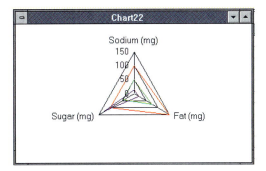

Figure 3-6: The fourth radar chart format.

category. I can't think of any good reason to use this radar chart format—except, perhaps, when the gridline actually communicates information. For example, if the first gridline happened to be, say, 50 percent of the daily dietary allowance, and the second gridline happened to be 100 percent of the daily dietary allowance, the gridlines just might be a useful tool for communicating more information and constructing a more interesting chart.

Radar Chart Format 5: A Radar Chart with Logarithmic Axes

The fifth and final radar chart format uses logarithmic scaling of the value axes, as shown in Figure 3-7. The only reason I can think of for using logarithmic scaling in a radar chart is if you're plotting a data set with a large range from the mini-

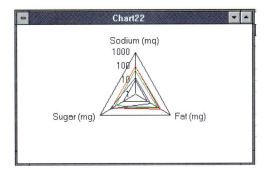

Figure 3-7: The fifth radar chart format.

mum to the maximum data point values. In this case, without logarithmic scaling, the smallest values in your data set would all appear clustered around the radar chart's origin (which is zero, unless you've modified it). With logarithmic scaling of the value axes, however, you can sometimes spread out the plotted data points so they're all legible. Or, failing that, you can spread them out so that at least more of them are legible. The problem with using logarithmic scaling, however, is that your viewer must recognize that the scaling increments are calculated as powers of 10—for example, 10^1 (or 10), 10^2 (or 100), 10^3 (or 1000), and so on.

Radar Chart Strengths

The strength of the radar chart type stems from its unique ability to calibrate separately and precisely data points in different categories by using separate value axes. Because this chart type uses separate value axes for each category, it also tends to emphasize the data categories rather than the data series.

Radar Chart Weaknesses

The radar chart type is not without its weaknesses, however. As a practical matter, you can't—or least can't easily—compare data points in different categories because the value axes aren't parallel and don't use a common origin. You can only easily compare data-point values in the same category. If categories aren't related, of course, this isn't problem. If two categories are related and you want to compare them, however, you'd be better off using a bar chart.

Another problem is that because each category gets it's own value axis, you can't plot data sets with many more than half-a-dozen categories. To my way of thinking, in fact, a radar chart with six value axes is already too visually crowded.

However, you need to pick a value axes limit that looks right to your eyes.

Finally, using a chart type—like a radar chart—that people aren't used to seeing can present obstacles. It doesn't have to be a problem, though, if, after you introduce your viewers to the chart type, you repeatedly make use of it. However, for presentations where you've only got a few minutes, it may not make sense to spend your time educating viewers about the finer points of data graphics.

Radar Chart Design Issues

If you're going to use a radar chart, there are a couple of chart-specific design issues you'll want to consider. First, because Excel plots the first category's data-point values on the vertical, or 12 o'clock, axis, you may want to make the first category the dominant category (if there is a dominant category). For example, in the junk-food radar charts, you may want to organize your worksheet data so the dietary element that concerns your audience most is the first category.

Another design issue relates to whether you need both line and symbol data markers. Because a radar chart's lines cross the value axes at the data point values, having both symbol data markers and line data markers is redundant. In many cases, you'll find it possible to make your chart either more interesting with additional data or more legible with less clutter by eliminating this data redundancy.

XY Charts

The xy, or scatter, chart is probably the most powerful and yet the least used chart type available in Excel. In an xy chart, Excel plots pairs of data points. In doing this, Excel lets you visually explore the relationship between two data series. It's with an xy chart, for example, that you explore the relationship between bond yields and bond maturities, the relationship between cigarette smoking and cardiovascular disease, or the relationship between education and personal income.

Figure 3-8 shows a worksheet that describes a farmer's experience with fertilizer. Column A shows the amount of nitrogen fertilizer applied per acre of farmland. Column B shows the bushels of wheat produced per acre. Figure 3-9 shows the same data presented in an xy chart.

Figure 3-8: Example data for an xy chart.

	A	B	C	D	E	F	G	H	I
1	Nitrogen	Wheat							
2	0	17							
3	1	24							
4	1.5	28							
5	2.25	34							
6	3.375	37							
7	5.0625	41							
8									

FARMER.XLS

Figure 3-9: The resulting xy chart.

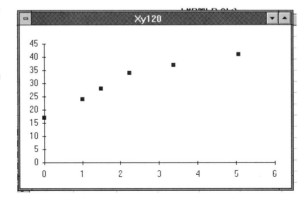

Xy120

Technical Tip

Exploring Relationships Between Data Series

The differentiating feature of an xy chart is that the horizontal axis is actually a second value axis used in plotting the data. This may sound complicated, but it's not. Let me explain. What you're really interested in doing with the data in Figure 3-8, is exploring the relationship between the nitrogen fertilizer used and the bushels of wheat produced. So, to do this, you create a plot area with two value axes: the vertical axis calibrates the dependent, or y, variable, which in this case is the bushels of wheat. The horizontal axis calibrates the independent, or x, variable, which in this case is the nitrogen fertilizer. To plot the first pair of data points—the values contained in the range A2:B2—Excel uses the y-axis and x-axis to find the point in the plot area that corresponds to zero units of nitrogen fertilizer applied and 17 bushels of wheat produced. To plot the second pair of data points—the values in the range A3:B3—Excel uses the y-axis and x-axis to find the point in the plot area that corresponds to 1 unit of nitrogen fertilizer applied and 24 bushels of wheat produced. In a similar fashion, Excel plots each of the remaining pairs of data points, again using the y-axis and x-axis.

By plotting pairs of data points using two value axes, xy charts let you visually explore relationships between data series. For example, Figure 3-9 shows that the bushels of wheat produced increases by using nitrogen fertilizer.

But you aren't limited to plotting a single pair of data points on an xy chart. In the case of the imagi-

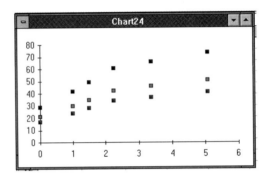

Figure 3-10: Three dependent variable data series.

	A	B	C	D	E
					FARMER.XLS
1	Nitrogen	Wheat	Barley	Oats	
2	0	17	21.25	28.875	
3	1	24	30	42	
4	1.5	28	35	49.5	
5	2.25	34	42.5	60.75	
6	3.375	37	46.25	66.375	
7	5.0625	41	51.25	73.875	

Figure 3-11: An xy chart with three data series.

nary farmer, you can visually explore the effects of using fertilizer on three crops—wheat, barley, and oats—by plotting three sets of data points, as listed in Figure 3-10's worksheet. Figure 3-11 shows the data from Figure 3-10 in an xy chart. The red data markers represent the pairs of wheat-nitrogen data points. The green data markers represent the pairs of barley-nitrogen data points. The blue data markers represent the pairs of oats-nitrogen data points.

The example described here uses the same x values for each of the data series. In other words, to plot the different yields, Excel always uses the same nitrogen fertilizer values—the ones in the range A2:A7. You can use different sets of x values, however, for different data series using the Edit Series command, which is described in Chapter 5.

*Table 3-2: XY
Scatter-Chart
Template
Descriptions and
Names.*

Description	Format	Regular Template	Slide Template
XY scatter chart with just symbol data markers	1	XY1.XLT	XY1S.XLT
XY scatter chart with both line and symbol data markers	2	XY2.XLT	XY2S.XLT
XY scatter chart with symbol data markers and horizontal and vertical gridlines	3	XY3.XLT	XY3S.XLT
XY scatter chart with symbol data markers and a logarithmic Y-axis scale	4	XY4.XLT	XY4S.XLT
XY scatter chart with symbol data markers and both logarithmic Y-axis and Y-axis scales	5	XY5.XLT	XY5S.XLT

Tip!

None of the xy chart formats provide a legend to identify your data series, although they will use the data series name as the chart title if the chart plots only a single data series. If your chart includes more than one data series, you may want to add a legend to identify the data series.

XY Chart Format Descriptions

Excel provides five xy chart formats. Table 3-2 identifies the five formats, and it also gives the names of the regular and 35mm-slide templates contained on the disk that accompanies this book.

XY Chart Format 1: An XY Chart with Symbol Data Markers

The first xy chart format, shown in Figures 3-9 and 3-11, just uses symbol data markers to identify the pairs of plotted data points. The first xy chart format works well when you want to emphasize the actual data points. The format, however, doesn't work well if your data series includes more than, say, four or five dozen data points, because the data markers will often begin to obscure each other.

XY Chart Format 2: An XY Chart with Symbol Data Markers and Lines

The second xy chart format just adds connecting lines to the first xy chart format, as shown in Figure 3-12. With connecting lines, the xy chart tends to emphasize relationships between the independent and dependent variables. However, if you choose the second format, you need to be sure your pairs of data-point values are arranged in the order of ascending or descending dependent variables. The reason this data organization is required is that Excel connects data markers with lines not in the order of the ascending dependent variables, but in the order they are arranged in the worksheet. Figure 3-13

Figure 3-12: The second xy chart format. Data-point values are arranged in order.

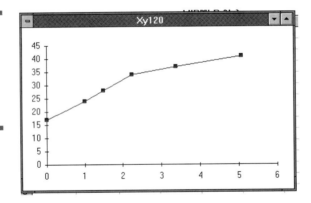

Figure 3-13: The problem of disorganized data points. Data-point values are not arranged in ascending or descending order.

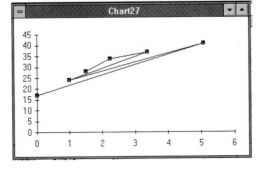

illustrates the effect of not arranging the pairs of data points in ascending or descending order, using the same data as that depicted in Figure 3-12.

XY Chart Format 3: An XY Chart with Symbol Data Markers and Horizontal and Vertical Gridlines

The third xy scatter chart format uses symbol data markers and then adds horizontal and vertical gridlines, as shown in Figure 3-14. With its horizontal and vertical gridlines, this format makes it easiest to gauge the plotted data-point values with precision.

XY Chart Format 4: An xy Chart with Symbol Data Markers and a Logarithmic Y-axis Scale

The fourth xy chart format uses symbol data marker and a logarithmic y-axis. As discussed Chapter 2, the value of a logarithmic scale is that it lets you plot the range of change in a data series' data points rather than the actual data-point values. By scaling the y-axis logarithmically (see Figure 3-15) this fourth xy chart format lets you plot the range of change in the dependent variable—the bushels of wheat produced—against the independent variable—the amount of nitrogen fertilizer applied.

Figure 3-14: The third xy chart format.

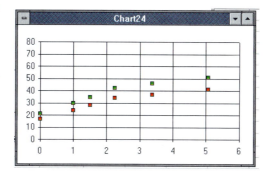

Figure 3-15: The fourth xy chart format. Initially, the rate of change in the bushels of wheat produced increases. Then, the rate of change plateaus.

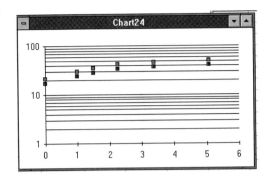

Figure 3-15: The fourth xy chart format. Initially, the rate of change in the bushels of wheat produced increases. Then, the rate of change plateaus.

XY Chart Format 5: An XY Chart with Symbol Data Markers and Both Logarithmic X-axis and Y-axis Scales

The fifth and final xy chart format uses symbol data markers and logarithmic scaling of both the y- and x-axes. Because of the logarithmic scaling on both axes, this chart format lets you plot the rate of change in the independent variable against the rate of change in the dependent variable. Figure 3-16 shows an example of an xy chart with logarithmic scaling of both the y- and x-axes.

XY Chart Strengths

The power of the xy chart format is that it lets you plot pairs of data points, thereby allowing you to explore the relationship between two data points. No other Excel chart type

Figure 3-16: The fifth xy chart format.

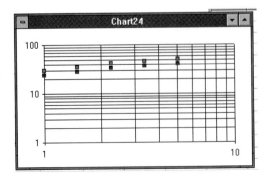

allows you to do this. In fact, by providing a visual means of exploring correlation, this chart type is (in the minds of most data analysts) superior to any of the other chart types.

XY Chart Weaknesses

There aren't really any weaknesses with the xy chart type, although it's easy to misapply the chart type. Specifically, it's easy to interpret a correlation between pairs of data series that aren't, in fact, correlated. The way around this problem, however, is simply to validate any correlation suggested by an xy chart using Excel's regression analysis tools. For information on using Excel's regression analysis tools, refer to the user documentation.

XY Scatter Chart Design Issues

There are just two type-specific design issues related to creating xy charts. I've mentioned both already. First, you need to arrange your pairs of data-point values by ascending or descending dependent data-point values if you want to draw lines between the symbol data markers. Figure 3-13 shows an example of the mess you will create when this rule is ignored.

Another point, which I've mentioned already, is that you'll probably want to validate any correlation between two data series using Excel's regression analysis tools. If you do perform this analysis, you may want to consider adding the least-squares line description produced by the regression analysis as an additional data series.

Combination Charts

Combination charts are not really a separate chart type. The simply combine two other chart types by overlaying one chart on top of another. The chart that is overlaid is called the *main* chart. The chart that overlays the main chart is called the *overlay* chart. All of this may seem like unnecessary confusion, but being able to combine charts by overlaying one type on top of another allows you to create a chart with two graphical data measures: lines and columns, for example. Or, you can create a chart with two y-axes—one that appears at the left end of the category axis and the other that appears at the right end of the category axis.

Because combination charts, in effect, combine two other chart types, you need to know how Excel splits the data series between the chart types. The basic rule is that Excel evenly splits the data series plotted in the chart between the two chart types that make up a combination chart. For example, if you create a bar-line combination chart using two data series, advertising expenditures and sales revenue, Excel plots the first data series—advertising expenditures—in the main chart using columns, and the second data series—the sales revenue—in the overlay chart using a line. Figure 3-17 shows an example combination chart that plots just this sort of data.

If you plot a data set with an uneven number of data series, Excel splits the data series so that the main chart plots one more data series than the overlay chart. For example, if you plot a data set with five data series in a column-line combination chart, Excel uses the main column chart to plot the first

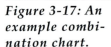

Figure 3-17: An example combination chart.

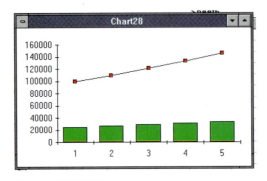

three data series and the overlay line chart to plot the last two data series.

Creating Combination Charts

You can create combination charts the same way you create any of the other charts. You can use the ChartWizard. You can use one of the combination chart templates provided on the accompanying disk. And you can create a combination chart from scratch.

You also have a fourth choice for creating a combination chart, however. And you'll want to be aware of it. You can create a regular chart. Then, you can use the Chart menu's Add Overlay command. In effect, the Add Overlay command splits the data series plotted in the chart in the active window so half are plotted in a main chart using the original chart type and half are plotted in an overlay chart using a line chart. You can't overlay a chart on top of a three-dimensional chart, however.

After you create a combination chart using the Chart menu's Add Overlay command, Excel changes the command name to Delete Overlay. Choosing the Delete Overlay command reverses the effect of the Add Overlay command, thereby returning the chart to its original chart type.

To change the chart type used in the overlay from a line chart to something else, you use the Format menu's Overlay command. All of the Format menu's commands, including the Overlay command, are described in Chapter 5, *Customizing Charts*.

Combination Chart Format Descriptions

Excel provides six combination chart formats. The two main features that distinguish the various formats from each other are which chart types are used to create the chart combination and whether the combination chart uses one or two vertical value axes. Table 3-3 provides descriptions of each of the combination charts, as well as the names of the regular and 35mm-slide templates provided on the accompanying disk.

Table 3-3: Combination Chart Template Descriptions and Names.

Description	Format	Regular Template	Slide Template
Combination chart with columns overlaid by lines	1	COMBI1.XLT	COMBI1S.XLT
Combination chart with columns overlaid by lines, with a second y-axis	2	COMBI2.XLT	COMBI2S.XLT
Combination chart with lines and two y-axes	3	COMBI3.XLT	COMBI3S.XLT
Combination chart with areas overlaid by columns	4	COMBI4.XLT	COMBI4S.XLT
Combination chart with columns overlaid by high-low-close lines	5	COMBI5.XLT	COMBI5S.XLT
Combination chart with columns overlaid by open-high-low-close lines	6	COMBI6.XLT	COMBI6S.XLT

Tip!

None of the combination chart formats identify the plotted data series. To do this, you'll need to add a legend, which you can do by using the Charting Toolbar's Legend tool.

**Combination Chart Format 1: A
Combination Chart with Column Overlaid by Lines**

The first combination chart format simply overlays a line chart on top of a column chart. As noted earlier, Excel plots half of the series in the data set using a column chart and the other half using a line chart. In general, you can use this combination chart format when all your data-point values are similar—for example, when all the data-point values are in the hundreds of thousands of dollars—and you want to emphasize the actual values of the data series plotted with bars and the trends in the data series plotted with lines. Figure 3-17 shows an example of the first combination chart format.

**Combination Chart Format 2: A
Combination Chart with Columns Overlaid by
Lines and a Second Y-axis for the Overlay Chart**

The second combination chart format again overlays a line chart on top of a column chart. And, like the first combination chart format, Excel plots half of the series in the data set using a column chart and the other half using a line chart. Accordingly, you would use this chart format if you wanted to emphasize the actual data-point values of the data series plotted in the main column chart and the trends in the data series plotted in the overlay line chart.

The difference between the first and second combination formats is that Excel adds a second value axis for plotting the overlay chart. This means you can plot data series with dissimilar data-point values. For example, you might plot money-market interest rates as decimal values and money-market fund flows in the billions. Figure 3-18 shows an example of a combination chart, with a column chart overlaid by a line chart and two value axes.

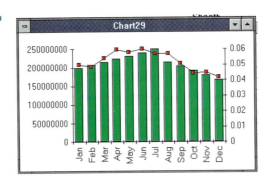

Figure 3-18: The second combination chart format. The left-hand value axis calibrates money-market fund inflows data-point values for the main chart; the right-hand value axis calibrates interest-rate data point values for the overlay chart.

If you tried to plot the data depicted in Figure 3-18 with a combination chart that used just a single value axis, the interest rate data points would all appear to be plotted as zero because the value axis would be scaled from zero to 250 billion.

Combination Chart Format 3:
A Combination Chart with Lines Overlaid by Lines and a Second Value Axes for the Overlay Line Chart

The third combination chart format uses the line chart type for both the main chart and the overlay chart. This chart format differs from a standard line chart, however, in that it includes a second value axis for the overlay chart. As mentioned earlier, the second value axis means you can plot two data series with dissimilar data-point values. For example, you could plot billion-dollar trends in money-market fund flows and money-market interest rates. Figure 3-19 shows an example of the third combination chart format.

Combination Chart Format 4:
A Combination Chart with Areas Overlaid by Columns

The fourth combination chart uses an area chart for the main chart and a column chart for the overlay chart, as shown in Figure 3-20. This format is well suited to those situations where you want to plot the trend of one data series against the data-point values in another series. Figure 3-20, for example,

Figure 3-19: The third combination chart format.

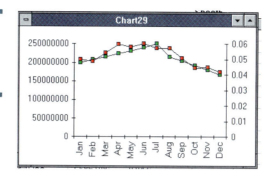

Figure 3-20: The fourth combination chart format. This format allows plotting trends of one data series against the data-point of another.

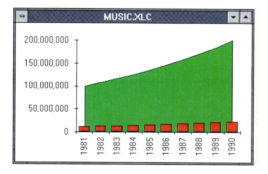

shows an area-column combination chart. You might use a chart such as the one in Figure 3-20 to show the trend in sales for an industry and the actual annual profits. The trend in sales, of course, would be plotted using the main area chart. The actual annual profits would be plotted using the overlay column chart.

Combination Chart Format 5: A Combination Chart with Columns Overlaid by High-Low-Close Lines

The fifth column chart format uses a column chart for the main chart and then overlays the column chart with a line chart, showing high-low-close lines. As noted in Chapter 2, high-low-close lines are most frequently used for something called technical securities analysis. This combination chart

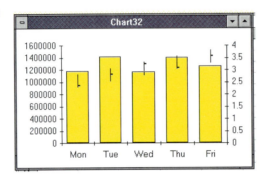

format is actually tailored for technical securities analysis. The basic idea is that you would use the main chart's columns to plot shares-traded volumes. Then, you would use the overlay chart and its high-low-close lines to plot daily share-price information. Figure 3-21 shows an example of this fifth combination chart. To color the columns, Excel uses the sixth color in the document color palette—yellow (if you haven't modified the palette).

If you don't understand the fifth combination chart format's high-low-close lines, refer to the discussion of the high-low-close line chart format in Chapter 2.

Combination Chart Format 6: A Combination Chart with Columns Overlaid by Open-High-Low-Close Lines

The sixth and final combination chart closely resembles the fifth combination chart format. It also uses a column chart for the main chart and then overlays the column chart with a line chart showing open-high-low-close lines. Again, this combination chart format is tailored for technical securities analysis. Typically, you use the main chart's columns to plot shares-traded volumes and the overlay chart's open-high-low-close lines to plot daily share-price information. Figure 3-22 shows an example of this combination chart format. To color the col-

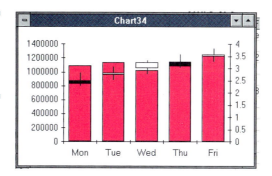

Figure 3-22: The sixth combination chart format.

umns Excel uses the seventh color in the document color palette—magenta (if you haven't modified the palette).

If you don't understand the sixth combination chart format's open-high-low-close lines, refer to the discussion of the open-high-low-close line chart format in Chapter 2.

Combination Chart Strengths and Weaknesses

Combination charts, of course, possess as their strengths the same strengths inherent in the chart types used for the main and overlay chart. For example, a combination chart that shows columns overlaid by lines gives you the ability to emphasize the data-point values using the column chart and emphasize the series trends using the line chart. In such a chart, however, the columns, because of their size, limit the number of data points you can plot. And, of course, the lines may suggest trends that don't in fact exist. In Chapter 2, I talked about the strengths and weaknesses of each of the chart types that are used to create combination chart formats, so I won't repeat that discussion here.

Let me say one other thing about combination charts. As you begin to work with them, you'll probably find they don't easily plot large data sets. The basic reason for this is that by combining different types of data measures—say, columns and areas—the chart's plot area becomes so cluttered it's impossible to clearly see each data series. In a combination chart that combines columns and areas, for example, you may need to look at the tiny gap between the columns to see data series depicted by areas.

Combination Chart Design Issues

You'll want to consider several chart design issues when working with combination charts. The first is probably obvious, but I'll mention it anyway. In a combination chart, you're really working with two charts: the main chart and the overlay chart. Therefore, you need to consider all of the type-specific design issues related to each of the two charts. If the main chart is a column chart, you need to think about column chart design issues. If the overlay chart is a line chart, you need to think about line chart design issues.

Tip!

There is a way to override the way Excel splits data series between the main and overlay chart. For more information, refer to Chapter 5's discussion of the Format menu's Overlay command.

A second design issue to think about is the way Excel splits the data series in your data set between the main chart and the overlay chart. Because of this, the organization of your worksheet data becomes important. Specifically, you need to organize your data series so the first half are data series you want plotted in the main chart and the second half are data series you want plotted in the overlay chart.

A final design issue related to combination charts is more subtle, but probably just as important. Needless to say, you should have a good reason for choosing to use a combination chart. It may be that your chart needs a second value axis to plot one or more data series. Or, it may be that your chart's message—for example, "interest-rate rise prompts inflow to money market funds"—is best communicated visually through a comparison of a trend in a line and the actual data in columns. But, when using a combination chart, you should be alert to its potential for misleading the viewer: Design variation within a combination chart makes it more difficult, and sometimes impossible, to compare two data series represented by different graphical data measures. An obvious example is when columns in an overlay chart obscure the data points that make up a line in the main chart. A more subtle example is when a chart viewer mistakenly compares the portions of a line or area between the actual data-points with the actual data point values shown in the columns.

3D Area Charts

A three-dimensional area chart plots data points using lines and then colors, or shades the area between the lines and the category axis. In a three-dimensional area chart, Excel uses the third dimension, or depth, in one of two ways: either it uses the illusion of depth to make the areas appear solid rather than flat, or it arranges the plotted areas in a front-to-back row. Figure 3-23 shows an example of the former.

As Figure 3-23 shows, Excel, by default, uses the category names—which in this case are the year numbers—to label the horizontal x-axis, which crosses the vertical value axis at zero. Typically, Excel scales the value axis—which is called the z-axis in a three-dimensional chart—so that it ranges from zero to slightly more than the largest data-point value. In a case

Figure 3-23: An example of a three-dimensional area chart. Excel uses the dimension of depth to make plotted areas look solid rather than two-dimensional and flat.

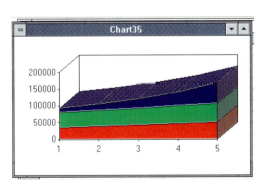

where the third dimension of depth is used to organize the data series, Excel uses the depth axis—which is called the y-axis in a three-dimensional chart—to describe the data series.

3D Area Chart Format Descriptions

Excel provides seven three-dimensional area chart formats. Table 3-4 summarizes the seven 3D area chart formats and identifies the names of the regular chart templates and the 35mm-slide chart template from the disk, which you can use to create area charts in each of the seven formats.

Table 3-4: 3D Area Chart Template Descriptions and Names.

Description	Format	Regular Template	Slide Template
Simple 3D area chart	1	3DAREA1.XLT	3DAREA1S.XLT
3D area chart with category-labeled area	2	3DAREA2.XLT	3DAREA2S.XLT
3D area chart with drop lines	3	3DAREA3.XLT	3DAREA3S.XLT
3D area chart with horizontal and vertical gridlines	4	3DAREA4.XLT	3DAREA4S.XLT
3D area chart using 3D plot area	5	3DAREA5.XLT	3DAREA5S.XLT
3D area chart using 3D plot area with horizontal and vertical gridlines	6	3DAREA6.XLT	3DAREA6S.XLT
3D area chart using 3D plot area with vertical gridlines	7	3DAREA7.XLT	3DAREA7S.XLT

Tip!

Some of the three-dimensional area chart formats don't identify the data series. If you choose one of these formats, you may need to add a chart legend, which you can do with the Charting Toolbar's Add Legend tool.

3D Area Chart Format 1:
A Sample Three-Dimensional Area Chart

The first three-dimensional area chart format just uses the third dimension of depth to make the area chart appear solid, as shown in Figure 3-23.

Supposedly, this three-dimensional area chart shows the general trend in Argentinean bauxite production and the general trend in total South American bauxite production. In reality, though, there's really no reason to use this chart in place of the equivalent two-dimensional area chart. In fact, by adding the illusion of depth, Excel only makes the chart more difficult to read. Notice, too, that this chart format doesn't identify the data series, so if you used it you would need to add a legend.

If you doubt my criticism of this three-dimensional area chart, look at the equivalent two-dimensional area charts in Chapter 2. With much greater clarity, they show overall trends in the first data series and in the total of all the data series.

3D Area Chart Format 2: A Simple Three-
Dimensional Area Chart with Category Name Labels

The second three-dimensional area chart format just labels the chart areas with data-series names, as shown in Figure 3-24. Unfortunately, this chart possesses all the serious problems inherent in the first three-dimensional area chart format because it doesn't use the third dimension of depth to organize the data it plots. As with the preceding three-dimensional area chart format, I can't think of any good reason for using this format in place of one of the two-dimensional area chart formats.

3D Area Chart Format 3: A Three-
Dimensional Area Chart Format with Droplines

The third three-dimensional area chart format adds vertical drop lines to the simple three-dimensional area chart format,

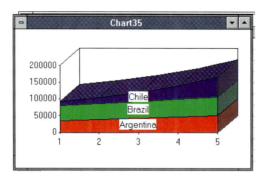

Figure 3-24: The second 3D area chart format. This 3D chart labels chart areas with data-series names.

as shown in Figure 3-25. With these drop lines, this area chart format shows not only overall trends in the first data series and for the total data series, it also shows the number of data points. Here again, the third dimension of depth doesn't organize the data. You would be better off avoiding this format and sticking with one of the two-dimensional area chart formats or one of the three-dimensional area chart formats that uses a three-dimensional plot area. Notice, too, that this format doesn't identify the data series.

3D Area Chart Format 4: A Three-Dimensional Area Chart with Horizontal and Vertical Gridlines

The fourth three-dimensional area chart format adds gridlines to the simple three-dimensional area chart format (see Figure 3-26).

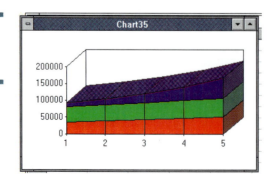

Figure 3-25: The third 3D area chart format.

Figure 3-26: The fourth 3D area chart format. With gridlines, it is easier to gauge the overall trend for the total data series.

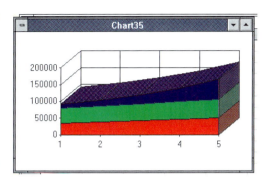

As result, this three-dimensional area chart format is marginally easier to read than the first three formats.

Again, however, there's no good reason to use the third dimension this way. The third dimension doesn't organize the data any better. And it doesn't summarize or describe the data any better. It just makes the chart harder to view. If you do choose to use this format in spite of these problems, however, notice that this format doesn't identify the data series. So, you'll need to add a legend.

3D Area Chart Format 5: A Three-Dimensional Area Chart using a 3D Plot Area

The fifth three-dimensional area chart uses the third dimension of depth to organize the data series, as shown in Figure 3-27. The first data series, for example, is shown in the foreground. The second data series is shown behind the first data series. The third data series is shown behind the second data series, and so on. To identify the data series, Excel puts data series names along the y-axis, which then becomes a data-series axis.

Of course, you don't need to use the third dimension of depth to organize your data if you're working with a data set that includes a single data series. A single data-series data set really has only two dimensions—the dimension of value that

Figure 3-27: The fifth 3D area chart format.

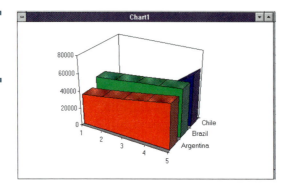

Figure 3-27: The fifth 3D area chart format.

is shown using the vertical z-axis and the dimension of category (usually time) that is shown using the horizontal x-axis.

In the case where your data is three-dimensional—which means it has two or more data series—the three-dimensional area chart format can be useful. If you want to plot bauxite production by country over time, for example, your data has three dimensions: production, which is shown with the value, or z, axis; time, which is shown with the category, or x, axis; and country, which is shown with the data-series, or y, axis.

The extra organizing power of the third dimension, however, isn't without its drawbacks. One of the first things to consider when you're using three-dimensional plot areas is this: If the data-point values in the first data series are large relative to the subsequent data series, the area of the first data series may obscure, or even hide, subsequent data series. Figure 3-27 plainly shows this. You can't see the first data points for the Chilean bauxite production.

This isn't the only problem with a three-dimensional plot area, however. With data series areas arranged in a stack of increasing visual depth, it's nearly impossible to compare values between data series. This means that a three-dimensional area chart works to show trends in the data series, but not to make comparisons between the data series. (If you wanted to compare the data series shown in Figure 3-27, for example, you would probably find a line chart more useful.)

3D Area Chart Format 6: A Three-Dimensional Area Chart Using 3D Plot Area with Horizontal and Vertical Gridlines

The sixth three-dimensional area chart format uses a three-dimensional plot area and horizontal and vertical gridlines. So, this format, like the one just discussed, uses the third dimension of depth to organize the data, as shown in Figure 3-28. To identify the data series, Excel puts data-series names along the y-axis. As mentioned earlier, this extra dimension of depth can be useful for presenting three-dimensional data, but it also causes some presentation problems. If the data-point values in the first data series are large relative to the subsequent data series, the area of the first data series may obscure, or even hide, subsequent data series. What's more, it's usually impossible to compare values between data series.

3D Area Chart Format 7: A Three-Dimensional Area Chart Using 3D Plot Area with Vertical Gridlines

The seventh, and final, three-dimensional area chart format uses a three-dimensional plot area to organize the data and vertical gridlines, as shown in Figure 3-29. To identify the data series, Excel puts data series names along the y-axis. As with

Figure 3-28: The sixth 3D area chart format. This format uses a 3D plot area and horizontal and vertical gridlines.

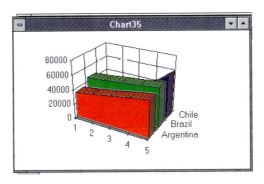

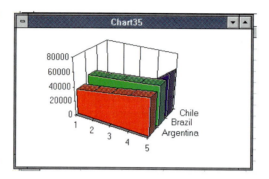

Figure 3-29: The seventh 3D area chart format. This format uses a 3D plot area to organize the data and vertical gridlines.

the other area chart formats that use a three-dimensional plot area, however, the dimension of depth may cause two problems. Large data point values in the first data series may obscure subsequent data series, and the varying depths of the plotted series make it very difficult to compare values between series.

3D Area Chart Strengths

As a data analysis tool, the strength of a three-dimensional area chart is that it lets you use another visual tool—the illusion of depth—to organize your data. This third dimension can be a useful tool for plotting three-dimensional data. Note, however, that this strength is true only of the last three formats—the ones that use three-dimensional plot areas.

Another strength of the area charts—both the two- and the three-dimensional varieties—is that they allow you to legibly plot many more data points than some of the other chart types. The reason for this, of course, is that the data points are simply points on a line. So even with the relatively low resolutions available on output devices like printers, you can legibly plot data series that contain hundreds of data points using an area chart.

3D Area Chart Weaknesses

Perhaps the most significant weakness related to the three-dimensional area chart type is this: the first four three-dimensional area chart formats violate a basic rule of data graphics—that is, your chart shouldn't have more dimensions than your data. All too often, the illusion of depth is simply used as a way to spice up or complicate an uninteresting graphic with boring data. A cursory review of your daily newspaper or favorite magazine will probably bear out this statement. Even worse, sometimes the dimension of depth is used in a way that makes it impossible to see one or more data series or to make comparisons between the data series.

Three-dimensional area charts also suffer from some of the same deficiencies as their two-dimensional cousins. For example, the lines and between-line areas tend to visually overpower the data point values. So, comparing data points is extremely difficult. And, without drop lines, it becomes next to impossible to know what the actual data-point values are, you actually know only that they fall somewhere on the line.

What's more, area charts may suggest trends that do not exist. A time-series graph, like an area chart, implies that time itself is a variable. But there are usually other independent variables that do a much better job of explaining any trends in the data.

3D Area Chart Design Issues

I don't want to sound like a broken record. I've already shared most of the problems and opportunities associated with three-dimensional area charts. Let me say, however, that the first design issue to consider is whether your data set justifies the extra dimension of depth. Clearly, any time you work with a single data series, your data set doesn't justify the extra dimension. And, even in a case where you're working with multiple data series and your data series represents a third dimension, you need to be sure that the problems associated with the depth dimension are outweighed by its organizing power. There's no hard-and-fast rule that people pass around or apply to make the trade-off determination, though. It all depends on your data.

There are also a couple of minor design issues you'll want to consider as you create and work with area charts. First, you don't need to identify the data series twice, so if you use an area chart format that supplies data-series names as labels, don't use a legend. Second, you can't use the area chart with drop lines if you're plotting large data sets because the drop lines become overpowering.

3D Bar Charts

Three-dimensional bar charts, like the two-dimensional variety, work well for comparing values in one or more data series, in something other than a time-series analysis. The reason is that each data point is plotted using a separate horizontal bar. Figure 3-30 shows more fictitious South American mining data in dollars. Figure 3-31 shows this data in a three-dimensional bar chart. The red bars show mining data for Argentina. The green bars show mining data for Brazil. The blue bars show mining data for Chile.

As Figure 3-31 shows, Excel, by default, uses the category names—which, in this case, are the mined minerals of gold, silver, copper, iron, and lead—to label the vertical x-axis.

Figure 3-30: More fictitious mining data.

	A	B	C	D	E	F	G	H
1		Gold	Silver	Copper	Iron	Lead		
2	Argentina	35000	38500	42350	46585	51250		
3	Brazil	45000	47250	50000	52500	55125		
4	Chile	12000	18000	27000	40500	2500		
5								

MINING.XLS

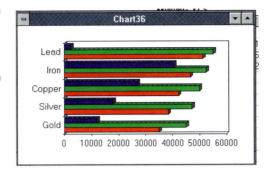

Figure 3-31: An example 3D bar chart.

Excel scales the value axis—which is called the z-axis in a three-dimensional chart—from zero (or from slightly less than the smallest value, if you plot negative values) to slightly more than the largest data point.

3D Bar Chart Format Descriptions

Excel provides four three-dimensional bar chart formats. Table 3-5 summarizes these four bar chart formats and identifies the names of the regular chart templates and the 35mm-slide chart templates on the accompanying disk, which you can use to create charts in each of these formats.

Table 3-5: 3D Bar Chart Template Descriptions and Names.

Description	Format	Regular Template	Slide Template
Simple 3D bar chart	1	3DBAR1.XLT	3DBAR1S.XLT
3D stacked bar chart	2	3DBAR2.XLT	3DBAR2S.XLT
3D stacked bar chart with 100% scaling of value axis	3	3DBAR3.XLT	3DBAR3S.XLT
3D bar chart with vertical gridlines	4	3DBAR4.XLT	3DBAR4S.XLT

Figure 3-32: The second 3D bar chart format.

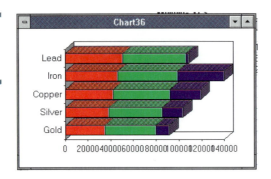

Figure 3-33: The third 3D bar chart format.

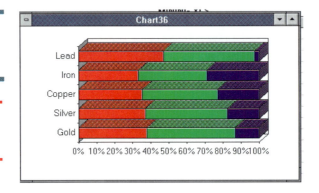

Tip!

None of the three-dimensional bar charts identify data series. If you want to identify data series, you need to add a legend, which you can do by using the Legend tool on the Charting Toolbar.

Figure 3-31 shows the first bar chart format. Figures 3-32, 3-33, and 3-34 show the second, third, and fourth bar chart formats. I'm not to going to spend much time discussing these four three-dimensional bar charts. All they do is use the third dimension of depth to make the bars look solid. That's it. Other than that minor visual difference, they are identical to the equivalent two-dimensional bar chart formats (formats 1, 2, 5, and 6 discussed in Chapter 2).

3D Bar Chart Strengths and Weaknesses
Compared to their two-dimensional equivalents, the three-dimensional bar charts don't possess any relative strengths. As noted earlier, all they do is make the bars on the chart look

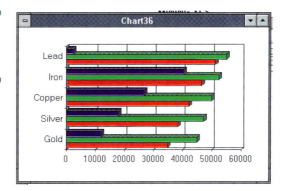

Figure 3-34: The fourth 3D bar chart format.

Figure 3-34: The fourth 3D bar chart format.

solid using the third dimension of depth. So, the extra dimension isn't used to organize the data. And it isn't used to give some new or different perspective on the data. Accordingly, there's usually no reason to use a three-dimensional bar chart.

One other thing of which you should be aware: by using the third dimension to make the bars look solid, the plotted bars can appear slightly longer because you see not only the side of the bar but also the end of the bar. This minor visual imprecision isn't always an issue, but if you're comparing two bars and one of the bars is very small, as shown in Figure 3-35, the tiny extra space used for displaying the end of the bar can make the bar appear larger. Compare the first red bar in Figure 3-35 with the first red bar in Figure 3-36.

Figure 3-35: A three-dimensional bar chart. The end of the first small red bar doubles its size.

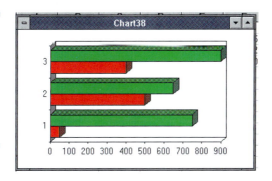

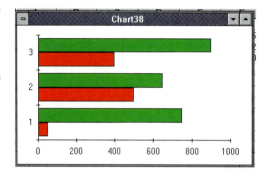

Figure 3-36: A two-dimensional bar chart.

3D Bar Chart Design Issues

If you decide to use a three-dimensional bar chart in spite of all my criticisms, you should know that all the same design issues that apply to two-dimensional bar charts also apply to three-dimensional bar charts. The main design issue for any bar chart concerns the organization of the data you want to plot. While there's a temptation to arrange data series or categories in alphabetical order, there's usually another order that makes more sense given the chart message—such as ascending or descending data point values.

Another thing to think about is the category names. You have room for much larger category names on any bar chart. In most cases, you'll want to take advantage of this bar chart strength to make your charts easier for people to understand by using descriptive, perhaps lengthier, category descriptions, rather than cryptic abbreviations or codes.

3D Column Charts

Column charts, including the three-dimensional variety, work well for plotting time-series data because people are used to looking at charts that use the horizontal axis to show time. On column charts, each data point is plotted using a separate ver-

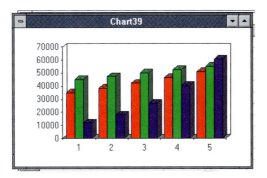

Figure 3-37: A three-dimensional column chart.

tical bar. Typically, data series bars are the same color. Figure 3-37 again shows the fictitious South American bauxite mining data, this time in a three-dimensional column chart. The red bars show Argentina's bauxite production. The green bars show Brazil's production. The blue bars show Chile's.

As Figure 3-37 shows, Excel uses the category names—which, in this case, are the year numbers—to label the horizontal, or x, axis, which crosses the vertical axis at zero. Typically, Excel scales the value, or z, axis from a minimum of zero to a maximum of slightly more than the largest data-point value. In the case where the third dimension of depth is used to organize the data series, Excel uses this depth axis—which is called the y-axis in a three-dimensional chart—to describe the data series.

3D Column Chart Format Descriptions

Excel provides seven three-dimensional column chart formats. Table 3-6 summarizes the three-dimensional column chart formats, and it identifies the names of the regular and the 35mm-slide chart template from the accompanying disk that you can use to create charts using each of the formats.

Description	Format	Regular Template	Slide Template
Simple 3D column chart	1	3DCOL1.XLT	3DCOL1S.XLT
3D stacked column chart	2	3DCOL2.XLT	3DCOL2S.XLT
3D stacked column chart with 100% scaling of value-axis	3	3DCOL3.XLT	3DCOL3S.XLT
3D column chart with gridlines	4	3DCOL4.XLT	3DCOL4S.XLT
3D column chart with 3D plot area	5	3DCOL5.XLT	3DCOL5S.XLT
3D column chart with 3D plot area with gridlines	6	3DCOL6.XLT	3DCOL6S.XLT
3D column chart with just X- and Y-axis gridlines	7	3DCOL7.XLT	3DCOL7S.XLT

Table 3-6: 3D Column Chart Template Descriptions and Names

Tip!

Three-dimensional column charts that don't use a three-dimensional plot area don't identify the data series. To identify the data series in these column chart formats, you need to add a chart legend, which you can do using the Legend tool on the Charting Toolbar.

3D Column Chart Format 1: A Simple 3D Column Chart

The first column chart format, which I'll label a simple 3D column chart, uses different-colored vertical bars for each data series. It also arranges the first data point set, or category, of each of the series together for comparison, the second data point set of each of the series together for comparison, and so on. Figure 3-37 shows the first three-dimensional column chart format. Argentina's mining production shows in red, Brazil's in green, and Chile's in blue.

Because Excel uses the third dimension of depth simply to make the columns solid, it's hard to come up with any good reason for using this format. You visually complicate the chart, but give the viewer no new information, nor do you provide any additional organization.

As is the case with three-dimensional bar charts, the extra dimension of the columns can be misleading. As described in the discussion of the three-dimensional bar chart's strengths and weaknesses, using the third dimension to make columns look solid can also make them look taller. This minor visual imprecision isn't always an issue, but if you're comparing two bars and one of the bars is very small, the tiny extra space used for displaying the top of the column becomes significant.

3D Column Chart Format 2: A 3D Stacked Column Chart

The second three-dimensional column chart format is the stacked column chart. This chart format just stacks the bars that make up the graph, as shown in Figure 3-38. You use stacked column charts when data points, whose bars get stacked, add up to a meaningful total, and you want see how a data point value relates to the total. For situations where you have only a handful of data points, stacked column charts make it easy to compare category totals and show how the val-

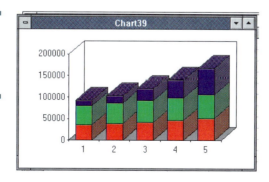

Figure 3-38: The second 3D column chart format.

ues of each data series relate to the total. With the South American bauxite production data, for example, stacking the bars gives you both a visual indication of the total South American bauxite production and also shows each country's production as a share of the total production.

Because Excel uses the third dimension of depth simply to make the columns solid rather than to better organize the data, however, it's hard to provide any good reason for using this format. What's more (mentioned earlier), the extra dimension of the columns can be misleading because using the third dimension to make the columns look solid can also make them look taller.

3D Column Chart Format 3: A 3D Stacked Column Chart with 100 Percent Scaling of the Y-axis

The third three-dimensional column chart format is a 100 percent stacked 3D column chart. It shows data points as percentages of the category total, making it easier to compare the sizes of the data points in a category. Figure 3-39 shows the same data as Figure 3-38, except this time the chart is the 100 percent stacked 3D column chart. I won't belabor the point about how this chart format doesn't use the third dimension for better organizing of the data.

Figure 3-39: The third 3D column chart format.

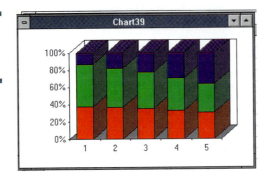

3D Column Chart Format 4:
A 3D Column Chart with Gridlines

The fourth three-dimensional column just adds gridlines to the first simple 3D column chart format. Figure 3-40 shows an example of the fourth three-dimensional column chart format. These gridlines may make it easier, of course, for your viewers to calibrate the columns.

3D Column Chart Format 5:
A 3D Column Chart Using a 3D Plot Area

The fifth three-dimensional column finally puts its third dimension to good use by organizing the data series, as shown in Figure 3-41. The columns of the first data series, for exam-

Figure 3-40: The fourth 3D column chart format. Adding gridlines may enable your viewer to calibrate the columns.

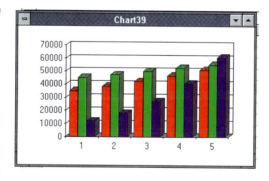

Figure 3-41: The fifth 3D column chart format. To identify which data series a row of columns plots, Excel puts data-series names along the y-axis, which becomes a data-series axis.

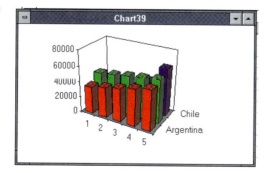

ple, are shown in the foreground. The columns of the second data series are shown behind the first data series. The columns of the third data series are shown behind the second data series, and so on.

The extra organizing power of the third dimension, however, isn't without its drawbacks. Two potential problems exist. One is that if the data-point values in the first data series are large relative to the subsequent data series, the first data series columns may hide subsequent data series columns. Figure 3-41 plainly shows this. Another potential problem with a three-dimensional plot area is that while you can compare values within a data series, you'll find it nearly impossible to compare values between two different data series because of the varying depths used in a three-dimensional plot area.

Of course, you don't need to use the third dimension of depth to organize your data if you're working with a data set that includes a single data series. A single data series data set has only two dimensions—the dimension of value, which is shown using the vertical z-axis, and the dimension of category (usually time), which is shown using the horizontal x-axis.

3D Column Chart Format 6: A 3D Column Chart Using a 3D Plot Area and Value-Axis, Category Axis, and Data-Series Axis Gridlines

Figure 3-42 shows an example of the sixth three-dimensional column chart format. The only difference between it and the fifth three-dimensional column chart format is that it adds gridlines for all three axes: the value axis, the category axis, and the data-series axis. The value-axis gridlines, of course, may make it easier to calibrate the chart's bars. The other two axes, however, don't really serve any purpose; it's easy enough without them to tell which columns are in which categories or data series.

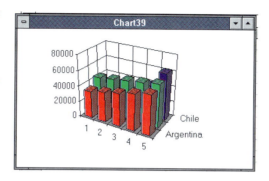

Figure 3-42: The sixth 3D column chart format.

3D Column Chart Format 7:
A 3D Column Chart Using a 3D Plot Area
with Category-Axis and Data-Series Axis Gridlines

The seventh three-dimensional column chart format closely resembles the sixth format. In fact, the only difference between the two formats is that the seventh format doesn't have the value-axis gridlines. As Figure 3-43 shows, it only has the category axis and the data-series-axis gridlines. These two gridlines don't really serve any purpose, however, because it's easy to tell in which categories or series a column is.

3D Column Chart Strengths

Three-dimensional column charts, like the two-dimensional variety, work extremely well for making whole-item to whole-

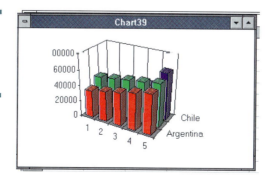

Figure 3-43: The seventh 3D column chart format.

item data comparisons when the categories are time periods. Each data point is represented by a single data marker—a column. Because of this, it's easy to identify, calibrate, and compare the data-point values.

Another strength relates to the orientation of the chart type. With the horizontal categories axis, column chart categories are easily used to show the passage of time.

Finally, if you use the third-dimension of depth to organize your data, a three-dimensional column chart may also make it easier for viewers to identify the data series.

3D Column Chart Weaknesses

Predictably, however, three-dimensional column charts are not without their weaknesses. First of all, Excel allocates space for the bars on the vertical, categories axis based on the number of data points. The greater the number of data points, of course, the narrower the columns. So, even with a relatively small amount of data, your column chart quickly becomes cluttered and, sometimes even worse, illegible. (This is particularly true of the column chart formats that don't use a three-dimensional plot area.)

Because there's less room for category names under the category axis, it's usually harder to clearly identify categories in column charts as compared to, say, bar charts. In a 12 month time series, for example, you won't have room to neatly fit the full month names: January, February, March, and so on.

As is the case with other time-series charts, of course, column charts may suggest trends that do not exist. The basic problem is that a time-series plot, such as a column chart graph, suggests that time itself is a variable, but there are usually other independent variables that better explain any trends in the data.

Tip!

You may be able to get around this space limitation by changing the typeface point size or the orientation of the category names. Both techniques are described in Chapter 5, **Customizing Your Charts.**

The stacked column chart formats possess another weakness. While you can easily calibrate the bars of the first data series because they abut the category axis, you can't do the same thing for the second and subsequent data-point values. The reason, of course, is that these subsequent data series bars abut against the preceding data series bars—and not the category axis.

Three-dimensional column charts also have a couple of weaknesses specifically related to their third dimension. First, the third dimension used to make columns look solid also makes them look taller. Second, if the dimension of depth is used to organize your data series, you can't easily compare columns in different data series because Excel arranges of the columns each data series at different visual depths.

3D Column Chart Design Issues

When you're thinking about three-dimensional column charts, the first design issue to consider is whether your data set justifies the extra dimension of depth. Clearly, any time you're working with a single data series, your data set doesn't justify the extra dimension. And, even in a case where you're working with multiple data series, you need to be sure that the problems involved with the depth dimension are outweighed by its organizing power.

Remember, too, when you work with three-dimensional column charts that use three-dimensional plot areas, you should usually place the smallest data series first, the next-smallest data series second, and so forth. This way, the shorter columns appear in the front of the taller columns.

The basic structure of both the two-dimensional and three-dimensional column chart formats also suggests several design conventions. You'll probably want to use column charts solely for time-series plots because a horizontal category usually shows the passage of time. What's more, you'll also want to use category names as short as people can easily understand them, because the categories axis doesn't provide much space.

Finally, keep in mind that when your data series includes a great many data points, a three-dimensional column chart becomes visually similar to a three-dimensional area chart. When you're working with three-dimensional column charts that contain a great many data points, therefore, you'll want to consider the same design issues as you do for three-dimensional area charts.

3D Line Charts

Three-dimensional line charts may work well when you've got a large data set to plot, especially when your data series includes many data points. The 3D line charts may also be useful for showing time-series trends and for highlighting simple relationships between the plotted data series.

Figure 3-44 shows a sample three-dimensional line chart, plotting sales revenue for two competitors, Acorn and Mammoth. The ribbon line for the first data series—that for Acorn—appears in the foreground. The ribbon line for the second data series—that for Mammoth—appears in the background behind

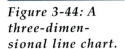

Figure 3-44: A three-dimensional line chart.

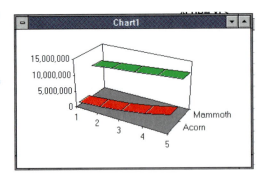

the first data series. If there was a third data series, of course, its ribbon line would appear behind the second series ribbon line.

To create a three-dimensional line, Excel plots the data points and then draws ribbon lines between each data series' data points. To differentiate the data series, Excel uses different-colored ribbon lines.

As Figure 3-44 shows, Excel uses the category names—in this case, year numbers—to label the horizontal, or x, axis, which crosses the vertical axis at zero. Excel scales the value, or z, axis so it calibrates the full range of plotted data points. In each of the three-dimensional line chart formats, Excel uses the y-axis to identify the data series.

3D Line Chart Format Descriptions

Excel provides four predefined line chart formats, as documented in Table 3-7. Table 3-7 also gives the regular and

Table 3-7: 3D Line Chart Template Descriptions and Names.

Description	Format	Regular Template	Slide Template
Simple 3D line chart	1	3DLINE1.XLT	3DLINE1S.XLT
3D line chart with 3D plot area	2	3DLINE2.XLT	3DLINE2S.XLT
3D line chart with X- and Y-axis gridlines	3	3DLINE3.XLT	3DLINE3S.XLT
3D line chart with 3D plot area and logarithmic scaling	4	3DLINE4.XLT	3DLINE4S.XLT

35mm-slide template names from the disk in case you want to create one of these three-dimensional line charts by using a template.

The first three of the three-dimensional line chart formats closely resemble each other. The only differentiating feature, in fact, is the presence or absence of horizontal and vertical gridlines. The first three-dimensional line chart format, shown in Figure 3-44, uses no gridlines. The second format, shown in Figure 3-45, uses both horizontal and vertical gridlines. The third format, shown in Figure 3-46, use only vertical gridlines.

While it may not seem like it from looking at Figures 3-44, 3-45, and 3-46, these three formats *do* let you compare (roughly) the absolute change in two or more data series. To make this com-

Figure 3-45: The second 3D line chart format.

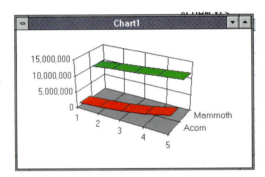

Figure 3-46: The third 3D line chart format.

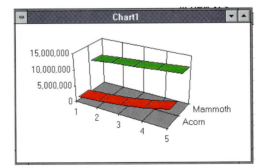

parison, however, you must focus on and compare the front edges of the plotted ribbon lines. And the formats with gridlines may make it easier to identify categories and series or to quantify values.

The fourth and final line chart format logarithmically scales the value axis. As I noted in Chapter 2, logarithmically scaling the value axis lets you plot the rate of change in a data series rather than the simple arithmetic change. Figure 3-47 shows an example of this fourth three-dimensional line chart format.

3D Line Chart Strengths and Weaknesses

In general, line charts—whether two-dimensional or three-dimensional—possess two main strengths: They let you plot very large data sets, and they emphasize the change in the data point values. Another noteworthy strength of the three-dimensional line chart format is that it uses the dimension of depth to organize and identify the data.

The strengths of the three-dimensional line chart type, however, are often more than outweighed by the chart type's weaknesses. Perhaps the most obvious problem of the three-dimensional line chart type stems from the fact that you must focus on the front edge of the ribbon line to see the plotted data point values. The problem with this need to focus is that

Figure 3-47: A fourth 3D line chart format.

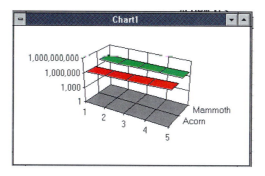

it unnecessarily increases the visual complexity of the graphic for the viewer.

There's another subtle problem with each of the three-dimensional line chart formats, however, and you need to be aware of it. Excel elevates the far corner of the plot area to create the illusion of depth. The trouble with this trick, however, is that it reduces the apparent positive slope of a ribbon line plotting a data series with increasing data-point values, and it increases the apparent negative slope of a ribbon line plotting a data series with decreasing data point values. This visual problem is most apparent when you look at the fourth format with the logarithmic value axis (see Figure 3-47). The actual data has Acorn's revenue growing at 50 percent annually and Mammoth's revenue growing at 5 percent annually. Yet this huge difference in the rate of change hardly shows up in the chart.

The line-slope problem is most serious for three-dimensional line charts with logarithmic-scaled value axes. For this reason, I can't think of why you would want to use the fourth three-dimensional line chart format.

3D Line Chart Design Issues

If, in spite of the attendant precision problems, you decide to use the three-dimensional line chart format, you should probably follow several design conventions. First, you probably want to use the chart type only for time-series graphs, since the chart uses a horizontal category axis. Over the last couple of centuries, people have grown accustomed to seeing horizontal axes to represent the passage of time.

Another point to remember is that the horizontal axis doesn't leave you much space for category names. So, in general, you'll want to use as short a category name as people can easily understand. In place of 1994, for example, you might use

94. In place of the month name October, you might use just the value 10, because October is the tenth month of the year. Excel uses the same formatting for category names as the worksheet cells containing your category names. So you can use worksheet formatting to control the numeric format of the dates used to identify categories.

3D Pie Charts

Three-dimensional pie charts, like the two-dimensional variety described in Chapter 2, show the relationship between individual data points and the total of all the data points in a single series. To do this, Excel draws a three-dimensional solid wheel, and then it slices the wheel into as many wedges as there are data points in the plotted data series. The size of a wedge, of course, depends on the data-point value and the total of all the data-point values in the series. Excel, for example, shows a data point value that's 25 percent of the total as a wedge equal to a quarter of the wheel.

To differentiate data points in the data series, Excel uses different colored wedges, explodes wedges, and sometimes labels wedges. Figure 3-48 shows sample data such as you might plot in a pie chart: South American bauxite production for 1993. Notice that pie charts plot only a single data series.

Figure 3-49 shows the data from Figure 3-48 plotted in a 3D pie chart. The red wedge shows the first data-point value, the Argentinean bauxite production. The green wedge shows the

Figure 3-48:
Example data for
a pie chart.

	A	B	C	D	E	F	G
1		1993 Bauxite Production					
2	Argentina	42350					
3	Brazil	50000					
4	Chile	27000					
5							

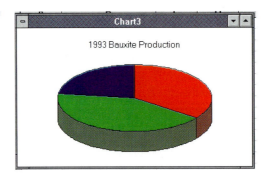

Figure 3-49: An example 3D pie chart. Excel positions the first data point's wedge—the Argentinean data point value—so it starts at the 12 o'clock position.

Brazilian data-point value. The blue wedge shows the Chilean data-point value. Wedges are ordered in a clockwise fashion. The second wedge abuts the first wedge's right edge. The third wedge abuts the second wedge's right edge, and so on.

3D Pie Chart Format Descriptions

Excel provides seven predefined three-dimensional pie chart formats, as documented in Table 3-8. Note that Table 3-8 also gives the regular and 35mm-slide template names from the disk in case you want to create one of these pie charts by using a template. As the format descriptions indicate, the two basic

Table 3-8: 3D Pie-Chart Template Descriptions and Names.

Description	Format	Regular Template	Slide Template
Simple 3D Pie chart	1	3DPIE1.XLT	3DPIE1S.XLT
3D Pie chart with data-labeled wedges	2	3DPIE2.XLT	3DPIE2S.XLT
3D Pie chart with first wedge exploded	3	3DPIE3.XLT	3DPIE3S.XLT
3D Pie chart with all wedges exploded	4	3DPIE4.XLT	3DPIE4S.XLT

Table 3-8: 3D Pie Chart Template Descriptions and Names (Continued).

Description	Format	Regular Template	Slide Template
3D Pie chart with category-labeled wedges	5	3DPIE5.XLT	3DPIE5S.XLT
3D Pie chart with percentage-labeled wedges	6	3DPIE6.XLT	3DPIE6S.XLT
3D Pie chart with category- and percentage-labeled wedges	7	3DPIE7.XLT	3DPIE7S.XLT

differences among the formats relate to whether Excel labels the wedges of the pie chart and whether Excel explodes one or more of the wedges.

The Problem of 3D Pie Charts

There's a critically important point to make about three-dimensional pie charts. The pie wheel is three-dimensional because part of the wheel appears in the foreground and part of the wheel appears in the background. This means that wedges in the foreground appear larger than the same-sized wedges in the background. When you consider this visual feature and the fact that the main purpose of a pie chart is to visually compare the sizes of different wedges, you can come to only one conclusion: Three-dimensional pie charts have no place in data graphic presentations. They are dangerously misleading.

For this reason, I'm not going to describe the three-dimensional chart type and formats here. If you want to use a three-dimensional chart anyway, let me point out that the three-dimensional pie chart formats differ in just one way from the two-dimensional formats discussed in Chapter 2: for the three-dimensional chart formats, Excel uses an oval shape with edges to give the illusion of depth. So, if you decide to use the three-dimensional chart type, you can peruse the discussion in Chapter 2 of the equivalent two-dimensional chart format.

3D Surface Charts

Three-dimensional surface charts represent Excel's most interesting and most powerful three-dimensional chart type. With a surface chart, Excel plots a data set using a three-dimensional surface. Figure 3-50, for example, shows data such as one might plot with a surface chart. In this case, the data is real and gruesome. Figure 3-50 shows cholera deaths over the period of a few weeks in London in the 1850s. The labels in column A and row 1 identify the major streets that intersect central London. The values in the worksheet cells show the cumulative number of deaths from cholera by city block.

I should admit here that my data is very rough. It's intended only to illustrate the three-dimensional surface chart, not to summarize the actual tragedy. To see the actual data, refer to E.W. Gilbert's article "Pioneer Maps of Health and Disease in England," in the *Geographic Journal*, 124 (1958), pages 172 to 183.

Figure 3-50: Cholera deaths by London city blocks.

	A	B	C	D	E	F	G	H	I
1		Oxford	Marlborough	Broad	Brewer	Piccadilly			
2	Seville	4	8	17	5	3			
3	Regent	7	23	43	37	17			
4	King	14	37	79	43	21			
5	Wardour	9	19	51	29	9			
6	Dean	3	9	9	7	5			
7									

CHOLERA.XLS

Figure 3-51: A 3D surface chart. Cholera deaths by London city blocks.

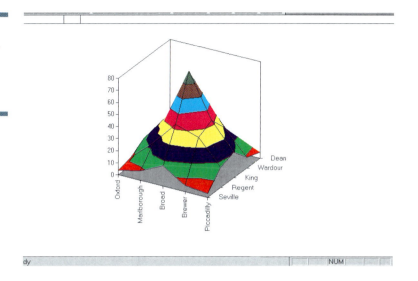

Figure 3-51: A 3D surface chart. Cholera deaths by London city blocks.

Figure 3-51 shows the same information, only graphically, in a three-dimensional surface chart. Interestingly, a London physician named John Snow actually plotted central London cholera fatalities using a chart. As a result, he identified the tight geographical concentration of cholera cases, concluded the deaths stemmed from the bad water that residents were drawing out of a public water pump on Broad Street, and stopped the epidemic by dismantling the pump.

3D Surface Chart Format Descriptions

Excel provides four three-dimensional surface charts. Table 3-9 on the following page summarizes and describes four surface chart formats, and it gives the names of the regular and 35mm-slide chart templates on the accompanying disk.

3D Surface Chart Format 1: 3D Surface Chart with Color

The first three-dimensional surface chart format, which is shown in Figure 3-51, plots data-point values on a three-dimensional grid and then draws lines through the data points

Description	Format	Regular Template	Slide Template
Simple 3D surface chart	1	3DSURF1.XLT	3DSURF1S.XLT
3D surface chart with wireframe	2	3DSURF2.XLT	3DSURF2S.XLT
2D color contour chart	3	3DSURF3.XLT	3DSURF3S.XLT
2D color chart with wire frame gridlines	4	3DSURF4.XLT	3DSURF4S.XLT

in each series and lines through the data points in each category. Excel uses your category names to label the horizontal, or x, axis and your data series names to label the depth, or y, axis. As with other chart types, Excel scales the value, or z, axis using the minimum and maximum values in your data set.

The most distinguishing feature of the first three-dimensional surface chart is how Excel uses color. On a three-dimensional chart type with color, Excel uses color to indicate the value-axis ranges into which the plotted data point values fall. These value-axis ranges are simply the major scaling increments of the value axis. In Figure 3-51, for example, Excel scales the x axis from 0 to 80 and uses increments of 10. Excel uses a different color for each range of data-point values. For example, data-point values from 0 through 10 appear in red. Data point values from 11 through 20 appear in green. Data point values from 21 through 30 appear in blue, and so on. When Excel assigns colors to a 3D surface chart with color (or to a 2D contour chart with color), it uses the colors in the chart document's color palette, starting with the third color in the palette—red. Excel starts with the third palette color because the first two colors in the palette are black and white. (Chapter 6 describes how to change Excel document color palettes.)

This is the most useful surface chart format because it communicates the maximum amount of information about plotted data. Looking at the chart in Figure 3-51—sickening as the data may be—you immediately sense the data's message: a tragic number of people in a specific neighborhood are dying of cholera. With the colored ranges, it's also relatively easy to calibrate the data at any surface location you can see.

3D Surface Chart Format 2:
3D Surface Chart Without Color

The second three-dimensional surface chart format is the same as the first format, except it doesn't use color to identify the value-axis ranges. Without the color, the lines that Excel draws between the data points in a category and the data points in series resemble a wire frame, or mesh. Figure 3-52

Figure 3-52: The second surface chart format.

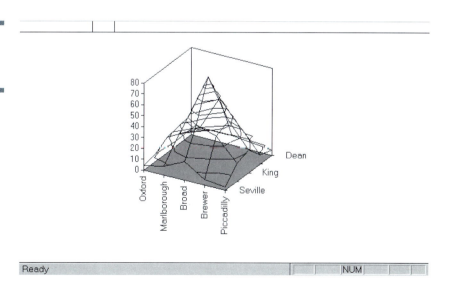

shows an example of a 3D surface chart without color. The chart plots the same data as does the chart in Figure 3-51.

3D Surface Chart Format 3: 2D Color Contour Chart

The third 3D surface chart format doesn't look three-dimensional at all because it looks directly down on the surface chart. Figure 3-53 shows an example of this chart format, which Excel calls a 2D color contour chart. Notice that by looking down on the chart surface, you are able to see the entire surface area. With the colored ranges, you can get an idea of the plotted data points—but only an idea. When Excel draws a 2D color contour chart, it doesn't display the value axis because you are looking down on it. So, in practice, what you would probably do is flip between this surface chart format and the first or second surface chart formats.

Because a 2D color contour chart doesn't display the value axis, it uses a number of colored value ranges equal to the number of data categories minus one. This is why, in Figure 3-53, for example, Excel uses four colors and not the eight colors shown in Figure 3-51.

Figure 3-53: The third surface chart format.

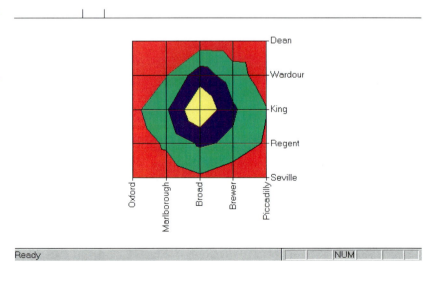

3D Surface Chart Format 4:
2D Contour Chart Without Color

The fourth and final three-dimensional surface chart format is the same as the third format, except it doesn't use color to identify the value ranges. Figure 3-54 shows the same data as Figures 3-51, 3-52, and 3-53, only this time in a 2D contour chart without color. Notice the similarity between Figures 3-53 and 3-54. The only difference is that Figure 3-54 lacks color.

3D Surface Chart Strengths

By drawing lines between both the data points in a series as well as the data points in a category, a three-dimensional surface chart lets you emphasize the relationships that exist both within the series and within categories. This, of course, means that surface charts are extremely powerful for plotting trends in three-dimensional data. You can even use surface charts to create rough data maps, as I did in Figures 3-51 through 3-54, simply by using your categories and series to represent differing latitude and longitude coordinates.

Figure 3-54: The fourth surface chart format.

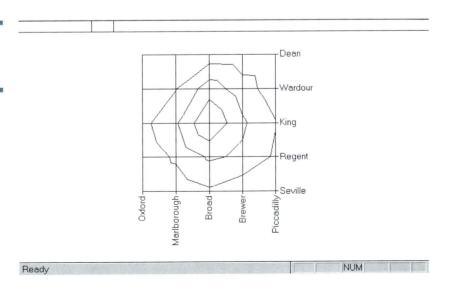

This characteristic can also be true of three-dimensional column charts if they use a three-dimensional plot area. Surface charts are, however, better suited to the purpose because they do not emphasize your data series, but rather use both your data series and categories as just different views of the data.

3D Surface Chart Weaknesses

Surface charts, like every chart type, do possess some weaknesses. As a quick review of the surface chart figures shows, it's easy for part of the plotted surface area to be hidden. You can work around this problem by flipping between the different surface chart formats, but this entails extra work for both you and your computer. With large data sets, as I've mentioned before, even a very fast computer may take several seconds or even minutes to draw your charts.

You should also know that some people suggest there's a problem with using color to indicate magnitude because there's no generally agreed upon order for color. Is red "bigger" than, say, blue? Is yellow "smaller" than magenta? You see the problem. In fact, if you look at Figure 3-53, you *really do* see the problem. Without looking at Figure 3-51 or 3-52, you can't tell which parts of the plotted surface show the largest data-point values.

Finally, the way Excel creates a third dimension and the way it gives the illusion of depth causes some of the same problems for surface charts as for the other three-dimensional chart types. For example, if your first data series includes large-data point values, it may obscure or hide subsequent data series. And you loose the ability to see precisely any trends suggested by the data series lines because Excel elevates the farthest corner of the plot area. In the case of surface charts, however, these weaknesses are often easily outweighed by their other strengths.

3D Surface Chart Design Issues

There are a couple of minor design issues you'll want to consider when working with surface charts. First, because Excel draws a line for each data series and each category, you successfully can't plot huge data sets with the first two surface chart formats. In fact, I think any time you plot more than around 50 data series or 50 categories, the wire frame that Excel uses to show the plotted surface area begins to look like a plate of black spaghetti. This threshold of illegibility, however, is just one man's opinion—mine. So, you should experiment and come to your own conclusions.

As far as the surface chart coloring goes, you may want to consider changing the Excel document's color palette so it works well for showing the magnitude of the plotted values. A monochromatic scheme—light blue, medium blue, and dark blue, for example—might work better than the Excel's default color palette if you can use the color change from lighter to darker blues to show a value chart from smaller to larger values. Or, you might try an achromatic color scheme—white, light gray, medium gray, dark gray, and so on, all the way to black—for the same reason. If you want to change the colors used in a surface chart, the way you go about doing this is to change the Excel color palette. Chapter 6, *More on Working with Excel*, describes how to do this if you're interested.

In general, the data-organization design issues I talked about for the other three-dimensional chart types don't apply to surface charts. You can't reorder the plotted data series, for example, if their order is part of the data. Or, returning to the London cholera deaths data map one last time, you lose the message of a surface chart if you arrange the data set so that the data series with larger values are plotted last.

Conclusion

The advanced Excel chart types described in this chapter open the door to a new world of graphic opportunities. The radar, xy, and combination charts let you plot more complicated and more interesting data sets. The three-dimensional charts, by adding the dimension of visual depth, let you plot data sets in a three-dimensional plot area.

With these powerful new tools comes a whole new set of potential problems, however. And this is particularly the case with the three-dimensional chart types. To successfully use these powerful graphic tools, one needs to be even more diligent in collecting and organizing data sets, in choosing chart types, and in selecting appropriate chart formats.

Let me say one final thing. I've spent a fair amount of time criticizing some of the three-dimensional chart types. Don't, however, mistake this criticism as criticism of the Excel product. Excel is an outstanding data graphics and analysis application. However, Microsoft, like any good software company, delivers the product features that users ask for. And if enough users ask for something—even if it's a dumb feature like three-dimensional pie charts—there's a good chance the feature will eventually make its way into the product.

4

Drawing

Excel, with its Drawing tools, lets you draw almost anything you possess the artistic skill to sketch. The drawing
tools aren't all available if you're working with charts displayed in their own document windows. However, all the
drawing tools are available for enhancing charts embedded in
worksheets. In the pages that follow, I'll explain how you
access the Drawing tools and how you go about using them.
I'll also discuss two important data graphics design issues
related to using the Drawing tools with Excel's charts.

Displaying the Drawing Toolbar

Excel lets you draw lines and shapes on both charts embedded
in worksheets and on chart documents. To draw these lines

and shapes, however, you need to use the Drawing toolbar, which isn't normally displayed. To display the Drawing toolbar, follow these two simple steps:

1. With either a worksheet or a macro sheet displayed in the active document window, activate the Options menu, as shown in Figure 4-1. Then, choose the Toolbars command from the Options menu. Excel displays the Toolbars dialog box, as shown in Figure 4-2.

2. Choose the Drawing toolbar from the Show Toolbars list box. Then, select Show. Excel displays the Drawing dialog box, as shown in Figure 4-3 in the middle of the active document window.

Figure 4-1: The Options menu.

Figure 4-2: The Toolbars dialog box.

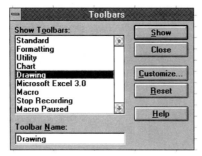

3. **(Optional)** To move the Drawing tools directly beneath the standard toolbar, drag the dialog box to the top of the application window. When you release the mouse button, Excel will display the Drawing dialog box as a secondary toolbar no matter what Excel displays in the active document window, as shown in Figure 4-4.

Tip!

Excel will display the Drawing toolbar until you remove it. To remove the Drawing toolbar, choose the Toolbars command from the Options menu so that Excel displays the Toolbars dialog box. Choose the Drawing toolbar from the Show Toolbars list box. Then, select the Hide command button, which replaces the Show button if the selected toolbar already shows.

Drawing with the Drawing Toolbar

As Figures 4-3 and 4-4 show, the Drawing toolbar is simply a collection of 20 command buttons. Table 4-1 summarizes the 20 Drawing toolbar command buttons. Not all of the command buttons let you draw things—such as lines, arcs, circles, and so

Figure 4-4: The Excel application window with a Drawing toolbar.

on. Some of the buttons let you modify the things you draw. You can use any of these Drawing tools in Excel worksheet documents, which means you can use any of them with charts embedded in an Excel worksheet. In chart documents, however, you can use only the Arrow, Text Box, Color, and Drop Shadow tools. I'll describe each of the Drawing toolbar's command buttons in the pages that follow.

Table 4-1: The Drawing Tools.

Name	Description
Line tool	draws a straight line
Arrow tool	draws an arrow
Freehand Line tool	draws freehand lines that take any form
Rectangle tool	draws empty rectangles and squares
Oval tool	draws empty ovals and circles
Arc tool	draws an arc or circle segment
Freehand Shape tool	draws a freehand shape, or polygon, which can take any form
Filled Rectangle tool	draws a filled rectangle or square
Filled Oval tool	draws a filled oval or circle
Filled Arc tool	draws a filled arc or circle segment
Text Box tool	creates a box into which you can type text
Selection tool	selects multiple graphic objects for editing

	Name	Description
Table 4-1: The Drawing Tools (Continued).	Reshape tool	changes the dimensions of a freehand shape (or line)
	Group tool	groups multiple graphic objects so they can be edited in a group
	Ungroup tool	ungroups previously grouped graphic objects
	Bring to Front tool	moves the selected graphic object to the top of a stack
	Send to Back tool	moves the selected graphic object to the bottom of a stack
	Color tool	changes the color of the selected graphic object
	Drop Shadow tool	adds a drop shadow to the selected object

Drawing and Editing Lines

The first three Drawing tools let you draw lines. The first tool draws a straight line. The second tool draws an arrow. The third draws a freehand line that you can shape any way you want. The Arrow tool works in both worksheet and chart document windows. The Line and Freehand Line tools work only in worksheet document windows.

All three of these line-drawing tools work basically the same way. First, you click the appropriate command button. Then, using the mouse, you indicate where you want a line and how you want it to look by clicking and dragging the mouse. Because each of the line-drawing tools operates slightly differently however, I'll briefly describe each.

Tip!

When you draw lines and arrows in worksheet document windows, you can force the angle of the line or arrow to 0 degrees, 45 degrees, or 90 degrees by holding down the Shift key as you draw.

To draw a straight line, click on the Line tool. Excel changes the mouse pointer to a cross-hair. Next, click on the point where you want one end of the line to be. Then, click on the point where you want the other end of the line to be. Excel then draws the line.

To draw an arrow in a worksheet document window, you follow a similar sequence of steps. First, you click on the Arrow tool. After Excel changes the mouse pointer to a cross-hair, you click on the point where you want the end of the arrow to be (the end without the arrowhead). Then, you click on the point where you want the beginning of the arrow to be (the arrow-head). Excel draws the arrow. The only thing you need to remember about arrow drawing is that it's the second mouse click that locates the arrow head end of the arrow.

To add an arrow to a chart document window, all you do is click on the Arrow tool or choose the equivalent command from the Chart menu—Add Arrow. Excel draws the arrow in the upper-left corner of the chart document window. To reposition the arrow, you move it, as will be described in just a few paragraphs.

Drawing a freehand line in a worksheet document window works only slightly differently. You click on the Freehand Line tool. After Excel changes the mouse pointer to a cross-hair, you click on the exact position where you want one end of the line to be. Then, you draw the line you want by dragging the mouse.

Figure 4-5 shows examples of all three lines—straight, arrow, and freehand. The lines are arranged in left to right order. To make the lines easier to see, I increased their weight using the Format menu's Patterns command. Chapter 5 describes this and other customization techniques.

Once you've created a line, you can move it. To move a straight line or an arrow, click on it with the mouse. Excel

*Figure 4-5:
Examples of
straight, arrow,
and freehand
lines.*

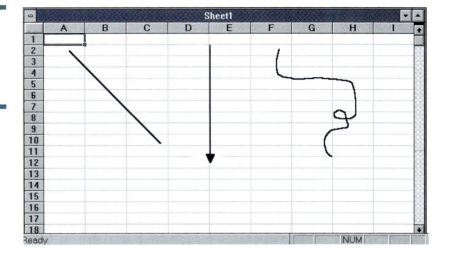

adds selection handles (which look like small, black squares) to both ends of the line to indicate that it has been selected. To move the entire line, point to the line and drag it in the direction you want it to go. To move just one end of the line—which will also change the size of the line—point the selection handle at the end you want to move and drag it in the direction it should be moved.

To move a freehand line, you also need to select the line by clicking on it. Again, Excel uses selection handles. With a freehand line, however, Excel uses the selection handles to draw the outline of a rectangle around the line with one selection handle at each rectangle corner and one selection handle on each rectangle side. To move the entire line, point to the line and drag it in the direction you want to move it. Or, to change the shape of the line, point to a selection handle and drag the line in the direction you want it to change. Excel, in this case, changes the shape of the line by either stretching it or shrinking it in the indicated direction.

Tip!

To move a line in only horizontal or vertical directions, hold down the Shift key as you move the line.

Tip!

If the active document window is a chart document window, only the Edit menu's Clear command is enabled. To clear an arrow from the active chart document window, select the arrow and then choose Clear. Or, you can choose the Delete Arrow command from the Chart menu.

You also have another method available for changing the size of a freehand line, the Reshape tool. To use the Reshape tool, select the freehand line you want to change by clicking it. Excel adds selection handles along the entire length of the line. To change the line, drag a selection handle in the direction you want to change that part of the line.

If the active document window shows a worksheet, Excel's Edit menu commands—Copy, Cut, Paste, and Clear—work with graphic objects like lines in the same way they work elsewhere in Excel. To copy, cut, or clear a line, all you need to do is select the line and then choose the appropriate command. To paste a line that was previously copied or cut, choose the Paste command. Excel pastes all graphic objects into the worksheet at the current location of the cell selector, so you'll need to use the techniques described earlier to move the line to where you want it positioned.

Drawing and Editing Shapes

Excel lets you draw more than half a dozen shapes in worksheet document windows, including rectangles, squares, ovals, circles, arcs, and polygons. In each case, you have the option of drawing either an empty shape (so you can see whatever is behind the shape) or a filled shape the color of the default background color, which is white. Drawing shapes in Excel isn't difficult, but there are a few tricks you'll want to know.

You can't draw any of these shapes in a chart document window. This means that these Drawing tools are really available only for enhancing charts embedded in worksheets.

Rectangles and Squares

You can draw rectangles and squares with the Rectangle and Filled Rectangle tool. To draw an empty rectangle, you click on the Rectangle tool. To draw a filled rectangle, you click on the Filled Rectangle tool. Either way, Excel changes the mouse pointer to a cross-hair. To indicate where you want the rectangle to be, click on the point where the top left corner of the rectangle should be positioned. Then, drag the mouse pointer to the point where the bottom left corner of the rectangle should be positioned. When you release the mouse button, Excel draws a rectangle that fits between the corner points you have identified.

Figure 4-6 shows two rectangles drawn in a worksheet so you can see plainly the difference between empty and filled shapes. The rectangle on the left is an empty rectangle shape: you can see the worksheet's gridlines through the rectangle. The rectangle on the right is a filled rectangle shape: it hides what's beneath the shape. Again, to make the shapes easier to see, I increased the weight of the rectangles' borders using the Format Menu's Patterns command. Chapter 5 describes the Format Menu's Patterns command, as well as other chart customization techniques.

You can use the Rectangle and Filled rectangle tools to draw squares, too, which are simply rectangles with all four sides

Figure 4-6: Two rectangles, one empty and one filled. This illustrates the difference between empty and filled rectangle shapes.

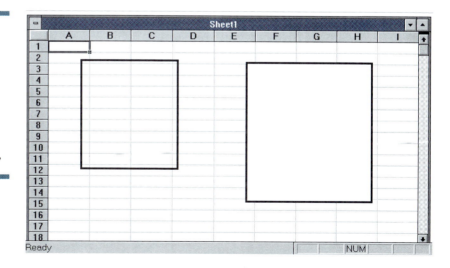

equal in size. To draw a square, just hold down the Shift key as you drag the mouse pointer between the two corners used to position and size the shape.

Ovals and Circles

The Oval and Filled Oval tools allow you to draw ovals and circles. Mechanically, the steps for drawing either of these shapes resemble those for drawing rectangles and squares. To draw an empty oval, you click on the Oval tool. To draw a filled oval, you click on the Filled Oval tool. Either way, Excel changes the mouse pointer to a cross-hair. To indicate where you want the oval, you draw a temporary rectangle into which Excel places either an oval or circle shape. To do this, you follow the same steps you would for drawing permanent rectangle shapes. Click on the point where you want the top left corner of the temporary rectangle to go. Then, drag the mouse pointer to the point where you want the bottom left corner of the temporary rectangle to be. As you do this, Excel draws the largest oval or circle that fits inside the temporary rectangle. Then, when you release the mouse button, Excel draws a permanent oval or circle inside the rectangle; then it removes the rectangle from the window.

You can use the Oval and Filled Oval tools to draw circles, too. To draw a circle, just hold down the Shift key as you drag the mouse pointer between the two corners used to position and size the shape. Figure 4-7 shows examples of an empty oval and a filled circle. Again, to make the shapes easier to see, I increased the weight of the circle's border using the Patterns command on the Format menu.

Arcs and Circle Segments

The Arc and Filled Arc tools allow you to draw arcs and curved lines, or circle segments. To draw an empty arc, you click on the Arc tool. To draw a filled arc, you click on the

Figure 4-7: An empty oval and a filled circle.

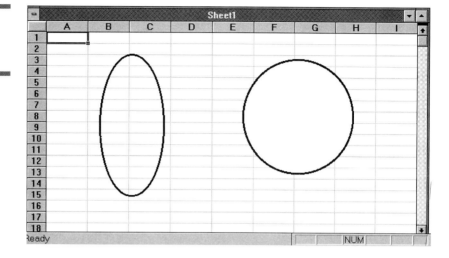

Filled Arc tool. Excel changes the mouse pointer to a cross-hair after you click on either Drawing tool. To indicate where you want the arc, you draw a temporary rectangle by clicking on the point where you want the top left corner of the rectangle to be and then dragging the mouse to the bottom left corner of the temporary rectangle. Excel draws the largest arc shape that fits inside the temporary rectangle. When you release the mouse button, Excel draws a permanent arc shape and then removes the rectangle from the window. Figure 4-8 shows examples of empty and filled arc shapes. I increased the weight of the arcs' lines to make them easier to see. To do this, I used the Patterns command on the Format menus, which is described in Chapter 5.

You can also draw empty and filled curved lines, or circle seg ments, using the Arc and Filled Arc tools. To do this, you hold down the Shift key as you drag the mouse pointer. Figure 4-9 shows an example of an empty circle segment and an example of a filled circle segment. Once again, I increased the weight of the lines of the circle segments to make them easier to see.

Drawing

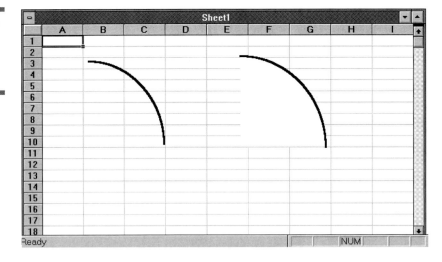

Figure 4-8: Examples of empty and filled arc shapes.

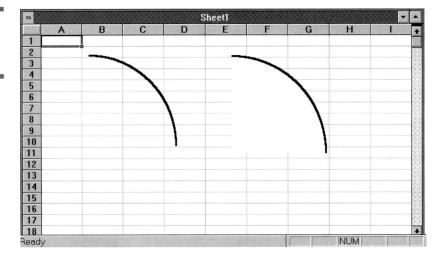

Figure 4-9: Empty and filled circle segments.

Freehand Polygons

To draw a freehand polygon what you really do is draw a freehand line and then connect the two ends of the line. First you click on either the Freehand Polygon or Filled Freehand Polygon tool. After Excel changes the mouse pointer to a cross-hair, you click on the point where you want one end of the freehand line to be (which represents the border of the freehand polygon). Then, you trace a line around the outside of the shape by clicking and dragging the mouse. To draw freehand lines, you drag the mouse. To trace a straight line so you can create a straight edge, click the mouse button at both the start and the end of the straight line you want to draw. You complete the freehand polygon when you connect the end of the freehand line that delineates the polygon border to the start of the line. Figure 4-10 shows examples of an empty and a filled freehand polygon.

Editing Shapes

You can move and edit any of the shapes you create using the Drawing toolbar's command buttons. To move a shape, for example, first select it by clicking with the mouse. Excels adds selection handles around the edges of the shape. (As noted earlier, Excel uses the selection handles to draw the outline of a rectangle around the shape, with one selection handle at

Figure 4-10: Examples of an empty and a filled freehand polygon.

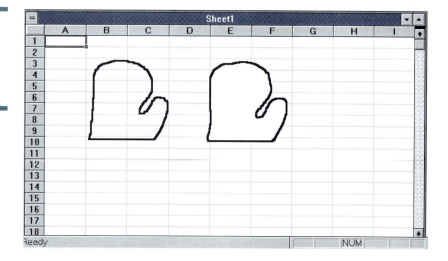

each rectangle corner and one selection handle on each rectangle side.) To move the shape, point to it and then drag it in the direction you want to move it.

To change the dimensions of the shape, you can use either of two available methods. To change a shape by stretching or shrinking it, you can point to a selection handle and drag it in the direction you want the shape dimension to change. This method of resizing, although available, is imprecise for freehand polygons. So, Excel also provides the Reshape tool. To use the Reshape tool, select the freehand polygon you want to change by clicking it. Excel adds selection handles along the edges of the shape. To change the shape, drag a selection handle in the direction you want that edge of the shape to go.

If a shape appears in a worksheet document window, Excel's Edit menu commands—Copy, Cut, Paste, and Clear—work with graphic objects like shapes in the same way they work elsewhere in Excel. To Copy, Cut, or Clear a shape, all you have to do is select the shape and then choose the appropriate command. To paste a shapes that was previously copied or cut, choose the Paste command. Excel pastes shapes into the worksheet at the current location of the cell selector, so you'll need to use the techniques described earlier to move the shape to where you want it positioned.

The Edit menu's Copy, Cut, and Paste commands don't work for chart document windows, however. For chart document windows, you can use only the Edit menu's Clear command. This command works in just the way you would expect. To clear, for example, a circle from the active chart document window, just select the circle and choose Clear.

Adding and Using Text Boxes

The Text Box tool, which you can use with both worksheet and chart document windows, lets you add boxes into which you can type text. The way you use the tool is simple and straight-forward. First, you click on the Text Box tool. If the active document window displays a chart, Excel adds a text box in roughly the middle of the chart window. Or, if the active document window shows a worksheet, you indicate where you want the text box by dragging the mouse between the box's opposite corners. To enter text into the box, all you do is type it in.

To change the dimensions of a text box, you use the same basic process that you would to change any shape's dimensions. First, you select the text box. Then, you point to a selection handle and drag it in the direction you want the shape dimension to change.

If you want to break the text apart onto separate lines, you can do so. To break a line of text in a worksheet document window's text box, just press Enter. To break a line of text in a chart document window's text box, press Alt-Enter.

Figure 4-11 shows a text box in a Chart window with the text broken into different lines.

Figure 4-11: A text box. You can break the text apart onto separate lines as shown in this text box.

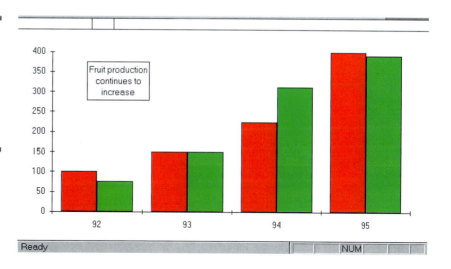

You don't have to enter text into a text box. You can also link the text in a text box to a cell on a worksheet using what's called an external reference. In this case, what the text box displays is whatever the worksheet cell displays. The easiest way to do this is to type an equals sign, click on the cell to which the text box should be linked, and press Enter. Following this method, Excel creates the link formula, or external reference, for you.

You can also type the external reference formulas yourself by typing an equals sign, the document name, an exclamation point, and then an absolute cell reference. For example, to retrieve text from cell A1 in a worksheet document named DATA, you type =DATA!$A$1. Working with external references can be a little tricky if you type them in yourself, so you may want to refer to the Excel user documentation for more information.

If you use retrieve text from a worksheet for use in a text box, there are a couple of things you should know. While normally, you can format the text in a text box anyway you like, you can't format text that is retrieved using a link. The reason for this is that Excel uses the same text formatting as the worksheet cell does. (Chapter 5, *Customizing Your Charts*, describes in detail how you format text box text that isn't linked. Refer to the Excel user documentation for information on formatting worksheet cells.)

Another thing to consider regarding linked text is this: the Spelling command, which appears on the Options and Chart menus, checks the text in the active document window. Therefore, if you retrieve text into a chart using a link, you don't actually check the spelling of the linked text by checking the spelling of the text in the chart window. To verify the spelling of linked text, you actually need to check the spelling of the worksheet document window that contains the text retrieved through the link. (Chapter 6 describes how you use the Spelling command to verify the spelling of all chart text.)

Colors and Shadows

With extreme ease, you can change the color of and add and remove drop shadows to lines and shapes. To change the color of an object, you select the object by clicking it, then choose the Color command button. If the selected object is filled, Excel changes the object appearance so it looks empty. If an object is already empty, Excel changes the color of the object to the first color in the document color palette—black. If an object is already the first color in the document color palette—usually black—Excel changes the color of the object to the second color in the palette—usually white. Subsequent use of the Color tool changes the object to the next color in the palette. If an object is the second color, for example, choosing the Color tool change the object to the third color—by default, red. If the object color is the last, or sixteenth, color in the palette, choosing the Color tool starts the sequence over again.

You can change the colors in a document's palette using the Color Palette command, which appears on the Options and Chart menus. Chapter 6 describes how you do this and provides tips for successful color schemes.

Adding drop shadows to shapes is just as easy. To do this, select the shape and then choose the Drop Shadow tool. Figure 4-12 shows the same chart window and text box as Figure 4-11, only this time the text box has a shadow. If a shape already has a drop shadow, you can use the tool to remove a drop shadow, too. Simply select the shape and choose the Drop Shadow tool.

Working with Multiple Graphic Objects

Because you can add many graphic objects to a worksheet document—lines, shapes, text boxes, and embedded charts—Excel

Drawing

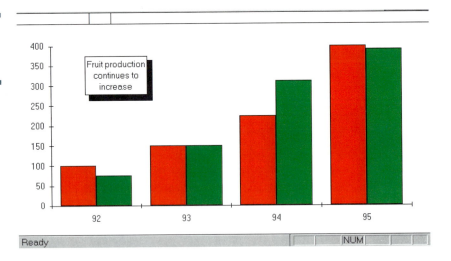

Figure 4-12: A
text box with a
drop shadow.

provides several tools for working with groups of objects: the
Selection tool, the Group and Ungroup tools, the Bring to
Front tool, and the Send to Back tool.

Selecting Groups of Objects

You can select a group of objects using the Selection tool. To
use this tool, select the tool's command button. Excel changes
the mouse pointer to a cross-hair. To indicate which objects
you want to select for the group, you draw a temporary rectangle around all the objects that should be included in the
group. To do this, you follow the same steps as you do for
drawing permanent rectangle shapes. You click on the point
where you want the top left corner of the temporary rectangle
to appear. Then, you drag the mouse pointer to the point
where you want the bottom left corner of the temporary rectangle to appear. When you release the mouse button, Excel
selects each of the graphic objects inside the temporary rectangle, removes the temporary rectangle, and adds selection han-

dles where the sides and corners of the temporary rectangle used to be.

Once a group of graphic objects is selected, any changes you make to one of the objects in the group affects all the objects in the group. For example, if you choose the Color tool, Excel changes the color of each of the objects in the group. If you drag a shape half-an-inch to the right, Excel moves all the objects in the group half-an-inch to the right. If you choose the Edit menu's Clear command, Excel erases each of the selected objects.

Grouping and Ungrouping Objects

You use the Group tool to tell Excel that you want the currently selected objects to be considered a single object. Once you group a set of graphic objects, Excel assumes that any changes you make to one of the objects in the group should also be applied to each of the other objects in the group. If you select one of the objects in the group, Excel selects the entire group. If you move one of the objects up, Excel moves all the objects in the group up. If you change the color of one of the objects in the group, Excel changes the color of all the objects.

To create a group of objects, first you select each of the objects you want in the group. You can do this by using the Selection tool described in the preceding paragraph. Or, you can do this by holding down the Ctrl key and clicking on each of the objects you want in the group. Once you select each of the objects you want in the group, you choose the Group tool.

The Ungroup tool, as its name suggests, simply ungroups a set of previously grouped objects. To use it, you select one of the objects in the group and choose the tool from the Drawing toolbar.

Technical Tip

Restacking Graphic Objects

In a worksheet, you can stack graphic objects on top of each other. This characteristic allows you to draw lines and shapes on top of an embedded chart. When you add a new graphic object such as a line, Excel positions the object at the indicated position on top of any existing graphic object. This doesn't mean, however, that you need to add objects in the same order you eventually want them stacked. The Bring to Front and Send to Back tools let you restack a pile of graphic objects once you've added them in. I should define a term: *pile* is the set of graphic objects that overlap each other.

The Bring to Front tool moves the selected object so it rests on top of a pile of graphic objects. To use this command, you select an object and choose the Bring to Front tool. The selected object is then moved to the top of the pile.

The Send to Back tool does just the opposite. It moves the selected object so it rests at the bottom of a pile of graphic objects. To use this command, you select an object and choose the Send to Back tool. The selected object is then moved to the bottom of the pile.

You can use the Format menu's Bring to Front and Send to Back commands in place of the Bring to Front and Send to Back tools. The commands work in the same way as the tools.

Drawing Design Issues

The Drawing tools described in the preceding pages of this chapter certainly can enhance the information you communicate in an Excel chart. And this enhancement can be particularly true in the case of embedded charts because all of the Drawing tools are available in worksheet documents. However, there are two extremely important design issues to consider. First, there is the possibility that these graphic objects may become phantom data markers. Second, the graphics don't usually contribute any new data.

Phantom Data Markers

The most important thing you'll need to consider as you add graphic objects to Excel charts is the problem of phantom data markers. Let me explain. A phantom data marker is simply a graphic object that a chart viewer either mistakenly or subconsciously interprets as actual data. In most cases, phantom data markers are graphic objects you've added using one of the Drawing tools. Figure 4-13 shows a simple example of this phenomenon. At the left end of the plot area, I've positioned a legend and changed its color to red. Given its position and color, some viewers might mistake it for a column in the column chart. It's probably even more likely that other viewers would subconsciously include the red legend box as a column in their visual assessment of this simple column chart.

Whether a particular graphic is or is not a phantom data marker is usually debatable. Does the legend in Figure 4-13 really mislead anyone? Does it corrupt the chart's message? To be honest, I don't know. I do think, however, there's a pretty good chance that it does mislead some people and that it exaggerates the increases in the plotted series data points.

There are different types of graphic objects that become phantom data markers for different types of charts. Text boxes and

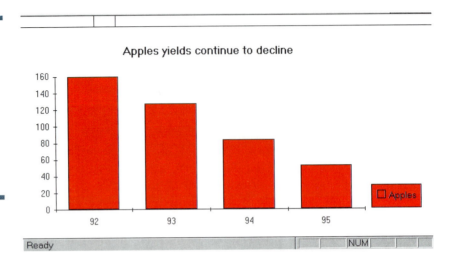

Figure 4-13: A column chart with a phantom data marker. The red legend box can easily mislead the viewer into thinking it is a column.

rectangles, for example, can become phantom data markers on bar, column, and combination charts because these chart types use, or can use, rectangular data markers. Lines and arrows can become phantom data markers on line charts, radar charts, xy charts, combination charts, and surface charts (with wire frames but without color) because these chart types use linear data markers. And arcs and freehand polygons, in some cases, can become phantom data markers on area, bar, column, and combination charts.

Shape isn't the only thing that causes a phantom data marker, however. There are other factors that encourage a viewer to mistaken or subconsciously see a graphic object as a phantom data marker—things like color, line direction and style, and the spatial relationship of a graphic object to the chart's real data markers. In Figure 4-13, the legend looks like a column because of its shape, border line, red color, and position.

So, what's the bottom line with this phantom data-marker business? Simply this: you must be aware of the potential for this problem so you don't accidentally include graphic objects that become phantom data markers.

The Problem of Nondata Graphic Objects

There's a second, more subjective problem with using graphic objects. The objects don't usually communicate new data, but they do attract viewer attention. Because of this, these nondata graphic objects distract viewers and may even obfuscate the data in a chart. This may seem like nit-picking, but remember that the purpose of a chart is to reveal data by summarizing, ordering, and comparing. If you add many nondata graphic objects—corporate logos, pictures, notes, arrows, and so forth—you detract from the actual data. What's more, if there's visual room for nondata graphic objects, why not use the room for adding more data, or more interesting data?

Conclusion

I don't pretend to be an artist. By training and experience, I'm a data analyst. Even for someone like me, however, Excel's Drawing tools are useful for enhancing its data graphics power. And I bet you'll find the same thing is true for you. You can add arrows that point out subtleties in the data. With text boxes, you can annotate your charts with additional information. And if you're an artist, you may even be able to go further—adding simple drawings, diagrams, and pictures.

5

Customizing Your Charts

Excel's 90 default chart formats provide you with a huge selection of chart type and format possibilities. These aren't your only choices, however. You can customize almost any aspect of Excel. This chapter describes in detail how to customize your charts. To easily use the information contained in this chapter, however, you need to know both the fundamentals of charting and about each of the Excel chart types. If you don't already have this information, refer to Chapters 1, 2, and 3.

Working with Preferred Chart Types and Formatting

When you create a chart without specifying the chart type and format—for example, when you select a data set and press

F11, or when you paste data into an empty chart window—
Excel plots the data using a default chart type and formatting,
or what Excel calls the "preferred chart."

Initially, the preferred chart is set to the first column chart format. You can change the preferred chart format, however. To
do this, display the chart type, including any formatting, that
you want to use as the default Excel chart. Then, choose the
Gallery menu's Set Preferred command. From this point forward, Excel uses whatever chart type you've identified as
"preferred" as the default chart type.

To redraw an existing chart—it could be any chart type—using
the default chart type and formatting, display the chart and
choose the Gallery menu's Preferred command. Excel re-draws
the chart in the active document window using the preferred
chart type and formatting. It's that simple.

Changing a Chart's Type and Major Characteristics

When you use a Gallery menu command to create a chart,
what you are actually doing is applying a standard set of chart
formatting decisions, including things like what type chart
will be used, whether data-series names should be used as
labels, how the value axis should be scaled, and so forth. This
approach is usually fine, but you may not want to do anything
more than simply change the chart type. When that's the case,
you don't have to use one of the Gallery commands. You can,
instead, just change the chart type.

I'm not going to describe Excel's chart types in detail here. I've
already done that in Chapters 2 and 3. You may want to refer
to those earlier chapters, however, if you want a quick review

of a particular chart type's strengths and weaknesses, or of type-specific design issues you'll want to consider

Changing the Main Chart

To modify the main chart type, use the Main Chart command, which appears both on the Format menu and on the shortcut menu when the active document window shows a chart. Either way, when you choose the Main Chart command, Excel displays the Main Chart dialog box, shown in Figure 5-1. (If you don't know what the main chart is, refer to Chapter 3 and its discussion of combination charts.)

Specifying the Chart Type and Data View

To choose a chart type, activate the Main Chart Type drop down dialog box. Excel displays a list of the 13 Excel chart types available: Area, Bar, Column, Line, Pie, XY (Scatter), Radar, 3D Area, 3D Bar, 3D Column, 3D Line, 3D Pie, and 3D Surface. Simply choose a chart type by selecting it.

Excel doesn't let you select a chart type that doesn't make sense. For example, if the chart you're rebuilding is a combination chart—a chart that consists of both a main chart and an

Figure 5-1: The Main Chart dialog box. You use the Main Chart dialog box to specify the main chart type and its major features.

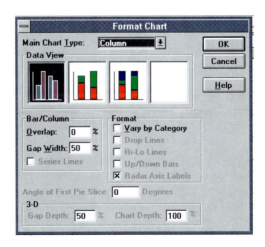

overlay chart—you can't select a three-dimensional main chart type.

Many of the chart types have different views of the data. The two-dimensional area, bar, column, and line chart types, for example, let you view the data as separated plotted series, as stacked series, or as 100 percent scaled series. The xy, pie, radar, 3D line, and 3D pie chart types provide only one data view. The remaining three-dimensional chart types provide three or four views of the data: separated plotted series in a two-dimensional plot area; stacked series in a two-dimensional plot area; 100 percent scaled series in a two-dimensional plot area; or separate plotted series in a three-dimensional plot area. If the chart type you select does have multiple data views, select the data view you want by choosing it from the Data View buttons.

The pictures on the Data View buttons are supposed to indicate how a certain view looks. Just in case you find this as confusing as I do, here's the general rule for interpreting the Data View buttons. In the case of two-dimensional chart types with multiple data views, use the first Data View button to indicate that you want to show each data series separately; the second Data View button to indicate that you want to stack subsequent data series on top of previous data series; and the third Data View button to indicate that you want to stack each data series and use 100 percent scaling of the value axis. In the case of three-dimensional chart types with multiple data views, you follow the same basic ordering scheme, except there's a fourth choice that lets you separately plot the data series in a three-dimensional plot area.

Type-Specific Design Changes

The Main Chart dialog box also lets you make several other main chart design decisions, including how bars and columns on bar and column charts appear and are organized, and how and where data markers and related graphic elements are drawn.

The Bar/Column text boxes and check box let you control how Excel draws the bars and columns on bar and column charts. The Overlap text box, for example, lets you specify whether the bars and columns in the same category overlap each other. You do this by entering the percentage of the bar or column width by which the bars or columns in the same category should overlap. Hence, an overlay percentage of 100 causes the bars or columns to completely overlay. An overlay percentage of zero causes the bars or columns to abut, so there's no space between them. An overlay percentage of, say, -50, causes the bars or columns to be separated by a space equal to the width of half a bar or half a column.

The Gap Width text box lets you specify how big a gap Excel should put between each category's bars or columns. As for the Overlap text box, you enter the percentage of the bar or column width. So, a gap width percentage of 100 causes each category's bars or columns to be separated by a gap that's as wide as a single bar or column. A gap-width percentage of 50 causes each category's bars or columns to be separated by a gap that's half as wide as a single bar or column.

Use the Series Line check box to tell Excel you want it to connect the bars or columns for each data series with lines. You can use this formatting option only with stacked bar and stacked column charts.

The Format settings let you control how Excel draws the data markers used to plot data points. For example, you can use the Vary By Categories check box to tell Excel that when plotting only a single data series, each data point's data marker should be plotted in a different color or pattern. This format setting, predictably, doesn't affect charts that plot multiple data series.

For these charts, Excel uses different colors or different patterns to identify the plotted data series.

Use the Drop Lines check box to turn the drop lines on and off. Only area and line charts have drop lines, so this format setting doesn't affect other chart types.

Use the Hi-Lo Lines check box to tell Excel to draw high-low lines between the largest and the smallest data points in each category. This format setting, which lets you create high-low charts, is available only for two-dimensional line charts.

Use the Up/Down Bars check box for a similar reason—to tell Excel to draw to the open and close boxes on a high-low chart. Again, this setting is only available for two-dimensional line charts.

The Radar Axis Labels check box lets you control whether Excel uses category names to label the axes on radar charts. Predictably, this format setting only affects radar charts.

The Angle of First Angle of First Pie Slice text box lets you indicate where Excel cuts the first data point's slice of a two-dimensional or three-dimensional pie. You enter a value equal to the degrees from the 12 o'clock position. So, a zero degree angle causes Excel to cut the first data point's pie slice starting at the 12 o'clock position. A 90 degree angle causes Excel to cut the first data point's pie slice starting at the 3 o'clock position.

The 3D settings control how Excel plots data in a three-dimensional plot area. The Gap Depth text box, for example, lets you specify the distance in depth between the different data series. You just enter a percentage of the data marker width. For example, if you want columns in a three-dimensional column chart to be half a column apart, you enter 50 as the percentage.

The Chart Depth text box works the same basic way, except it specifies how deep a 3D chart should be as a percentage of its width. For example, to tell Excel you want a chart just as wide as it is deep, you enter 100 as the percentage.

Once you've indicated the chart type, data view, and major chart attributes using the Main Chart dialog box, select OK. Excel makes your changes to the chart in the active document.

Adding and Formatting Overlay Charts

Most charts only have a main chart. However, as noted in Chapter 3, combination charts also have an overlay chart, which is simply another chart type laid on top of, or "over-laid" on, the main chart. You don't have to create and format combination charts using the Gallery menu commands, however. You can also use the Add Overlay and Overlay commands.

If you choose one of the Gallery menu commands, you lose any special formatting you've made to a chart, including the addition of an overlay chart. In effect, when you choose a Gallery menu command, Excel replaces all the existing formatting with that supplied by the chart format you select.

Adding an Overlay Chart

To add an overlay chart to the chart displayed in the active window, you just choose the Chart menu's Add Overlay command. Excel splits the plotted data series between the main and overlay charts, using a line chart for the overlay chart type. At this point, you can use the Format menu's Overlay command to adjust the overlay chart type and its dominant chart characteristics.

Formatting the Overlay Chart Type

To specify the overlay chart type and make other major changes to the overlay chart, use the Overlay command. The Overlay command appears on both the Format menu and the shortcut menu when the active document window displays a

Tip!

To remove an overlay chart so all a chart's data series are plotted on the main chart, use the Chart menu's Delete Overlay command. The Delete Overlay command replaces the Chart menu's Add Overlay command whenever the active chart document window shows a combination chart.

chart. When you choose the Overlay command, Excel displays the Overlay Chart dialog box, as shown in Figure 5-2.

To choose an overlay chart type, activate the Overlay Chart Type drop down dialog box. Excel displays a list of the seven available Excel chart types—Area, Bar, Column, Line, Pie, XY (Scatter), and Radar—and you select the desired overlay chart type. Excel doesn't list any of the three-dimensional chart types because they aren't available for use in combination charts.

Tip!

Just because Excel lets you combine two chart types doesn't mean that the resulting combination makes sense. For example, you can overlay a pie chart on top of another main chart type, but Excel places the pie chart in the middle of the plot area, thereby hiding part of the main chart. In my experience, it's difficult to successfully overlay pie charts, xy charts, and radar charts, which is probably why these chart types aren't used as overlay charts in any of the Gallery menu's combination chart formats.

As for with the main chart types, many of the overlay chart types have different views of the data. You can select the data view you want by choosing it from the Data View buttons. If a particular chart type has multiple data views, use the first

Figure 5-2: The Overlay dialog box.

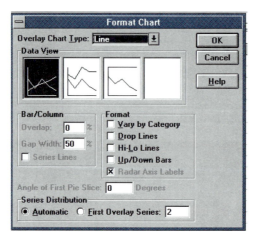

Data View button to indicate that you want to show each data series separately; the second Data View button to indicate that you want to stack subsequent data series on top of previous data series; and the third Data View button to indicate that you want to stack data series and use 100 percent scaling of the value axis.

Like the Main Chart dialog box described earlier, the Overlay Chart dialog box also lets you make several other chart-design decisions. These other settings work the same basic way they do on the Main Chart dialog box. For example, the Bar/Column settings let you control several aspects of how Excel draws bar and column chart data markers. The Overlap text box, for example, lets you specify whether the bars and columns in the same category overlap each other. The Gap Width text box lets you specify how big a gap Excel should put between each category's bars or columns. You use the Series Line check box to tell Excel that you want it to connect the bars or columns with lines for each data series in stacked bar and column charts.

The Format settings let you control how Excel draws the data markers used to plot data points. You use the Vary By Categories check box to tell Excel that you're plotting only a single data series and that each data point's data marker should be plotted in a different color or pattern. You use the Drop Lines check box to turn the drop lines on and off. You use the Hi-Lo Lines check box to tell Excel to draw high-low lines between the largest and the smallest data points in each category on a line chart. You use the Up/Down Bars check box for a similar reason: to tell Excel to draw to the open and close boxes on a high-low line chart. The Radar Axis Labels check box lets you control whether Excel uses category names to label the axes on radar charts. Finally, the Angle of First Angle of First Pie Slice text box lets you specify where Excel cuts the first data point's slice of a pie chart.

The Series Distribution radio buttons and text box are actually the only new settings on the Overlay Chart dialog box, compared to the Main Chart dialog box. Mark the Automatic radio button if you want Excel to evenly split the data series between the main and overlay charts. (If you plot a data set with an uneven number of data series, Excel splits the data series so the main chart has one more data series than the overlay chart.)

If you don't want Excel to evenly split the data series between the main and overlay charts, you use the First Overlay Series radio button and text box. To do this, mark the First Overlay Series radio button, then enter the number of the first series that should be plotted in the overlay chart. For example, in a combination chart with four data series, Excel normally plots the first two data series in the main chart and the last two in the overlay chart. If, instead, you want to plot only the last, or fourth, data series in the overlay chart, mark the First Overlay Series radio button and enter a 4 in the text box provided.

Adjusting the Three-Dimensional Settings

A three-dimensional chart looks three-dimensional because Excel adds the optical illusion of depth. As part of the illusion, Excel rotates a three-dimensional chart, elevates the far corner, and adds the perspective of depth, as shown in Figure 5-3. The default elevation, rotation, and perspective settings work fine as initial settings. However, you may be able to improve the visual precision of a three-dimensional chart by adjusting these settings.

To adjust the elevation, rotation and perspective of a three-dimensional chart, use the Format menu's 3D View command. When you choose this command, Excel displays the 3D View dialog box, as shown in Figure 5-4. Note that the 3D View dialog box includes a picture box that lets you see what the three-dimensional chart looks like as you make your changes.

Figure 5-3: An example of a three-dimensional surface chart.

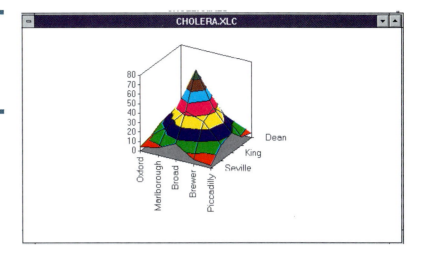

Figure 5-4: The 3D View dialog box.

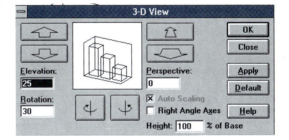

Degrees of Elevation

The degrees-of-elevation setting specifies the height from which you look at the chart, by quantifying the angle in degrees between the viewer's line of vision and the chart's floor, or main surface. For three-dimensional area, column, line, and surface charts, valid elevation settings range from -90 degrees, which means the viewer looks directly up at a chart, to 90 degrees, which means the viewer looks directly down on a chart. For three-dimensional pie charts, valid elevation settings range from 10 to 80 degrees. For three-dimensional bar charts, valid elevation settings range from 0 to 44 degrees.

To make elevation adjustments, use either the Elevation text box or the Elevation command buttons, which appear above the Elevation text box. The initial elevation setting is 15 degrees. You can increase this elevation by entering a larger degrees setting in the Elevation text box or by clicking on the Elevation command button with the Up Arrow. Or, you can decrease this elevation by entering a smaller degrees setting or even a negative degrees setting in the Elevation text box or by clicking on the Elevation command button with the Down Arrow. Each click of an Elevation command button changes the elevation by 5 degrees.

As a general rule, you increase the visual precision of a three-dimensional chart by adjusting the elevation of the chart to that of the equivalent two-dimensional chart. This means that area, bar, column, line, and surface charts become more precise the closer you set the elevation angle to zero. Pie charts become more precise the closer you set the elevation angle to 90. Unfortunately, the more precise you make a three-dimensional chart using the elevation setting, the less three-dimensional it looks.

Degrees of Rotation

The rotation setting specifies degrees of rotation of the x-axis around the z-axis. Pie charts, because they don't have an x-axis, can't be rotated. Area, column, line and surface charts can be rotated 360 degrees. Bar charts can be rotated from 0 to 44 degrees.

To make rotation adjustments, use either the Rotation text box or the Rotation command buttons, which appear to the right of the Rotation text box and beneath the picture box. The initial rotation setting is 20. You can increase the rotation by entering a larger degrees setting in the Rotation text box or by clicking on the Rotation command button with the clockwise arrow. Or, you can decrease the rotation by entering a smaller degrees setting or by clicking on the Rotation command button with the counterclockwise arrow. Each click of a Rotation command button changes the rotation by 10 degrees.

As a general rule, you increase the visual precision of a three-dimensional chart by adjusting its rotation toward 0 degrees. The problem, however, is that a three-dimensional chart with a 0 degree elevation angle and 0-degrees of rotation isn't three-dimensional at all. It's two-dimensional.

Depth Perspective Ratio

Tip!

You can also use the mouse to change the three-dimensional view of a three-dimensional chart. To do this, click on the chart's walls to select them. Then, drag the selection handles to adjust the elevation, rotation, height, and perspective.

With the perspective-of-depth ratio setting, you specify how much visual depth Excel uses for the chart. To specify the perspective-of-depth ratio, you enter the ratio of the chart front to back. A higher perspective-of-depth ratio gives the illusion of greater depth; a lower perspective-of-depth ratio gives the illusion of less depth. For three-dimensional area, column, line, and surface charts, you can choose perspective-of-depth ratios that range from 0 to 100. You can't, however, specify a perspective-of-depth ratio for a three-dimensional bar chart.

Auto Scaling

In general, Excel draws smaller three-dimensional charts than two-dimensional charts. You can tell Excel to draw three-dimensional charts that are just as large as their two-dimensional equivalents, however, by marking the Auto Scaling check box. The Auto Scaling option is only available if the Right Angle Axes check box is marked and the degree of rotation is less than 45. The Right Angle Axes option is described next.

Right Angle Axes

The Right Angle Axes check box, if marked, causes Excel to draw the axes at right, or 90 degree, angles, regardless of the degrees of elevation or rotation. This setting lets you more precisely calibrate data markers, but charts with right angle axes don't look as three-dimensional because they don't have a perspective of depth. For this reason, you can't specify a perspective of depth setting for charts with right angle axes.

Height of Base

The Height of Base text box lets you set the height of the z-axis and chart walls as a percentage of the chart's x-axis, or base width. A Height of Base setting equal to 100, for example, indicates that you want the chart height to equal the chart base width.

3D View Command Buttons

The 3D View dialog box also provides two command buttons, Apply and Default. The Apply command button uses the current 3D view settings to update the chart in the active document window without closing the dialog box. In other words, you can see (or at least partially see) the effect of your 3D view settings without having to close the 3D View dialog box. Note that by leaving the 3D View dialog box in the application window, however, you may have difficulty seeing the entire chart.

The Default command button adjusts all the 3D view settings back to their original values. Let me point out one other subtlety of the 3D View command, unlike the other chart design changes you make with the Chart and Format menu commands, you don't override 3D view changes with Gallery menu commands. So, you'll need to use the Default command button to return to the initial 3D View settings.

Data-Series Changes

You can change the data series plotted in a chart from the chart document window. For example, you can change the data series plotted in a chart, and you can change the name of, or the data points included in, a data series. To make these changes, you use the Edit Series command, which appears both on the Chart menu and on the shortcut menu.

Adding a New Data Series with the Edit Series Command

You can use the Edit Series command to add data series to an existing chart. To add a data series, choose the Edit Series command. Excel displays the Edit Series dialog box, as shown in Figure 5-5.

Mark the New Series item in the Series List box. Then, move the selection cursor to the Name text box and enter the name of the data series. You can enter a piece of text for the name, such as "Revenues." Alternatively, you can create a link formula that references a cell in a worksheet. In this case, Excel uses the label in the linked cell as the data-series name.

The easiest way to create a link formula is by clicking on the worksheet cell with the label you want to use as a data-series name. If you click on cell A4 in a worksheet named BUDGET, for example, Excel creates the external reference =BUDGET!$A$4. Alternatively, you can also type this link formula yourself.

If you don't provide a name for a data series, Excel creates one for you by using the word "Series" and the plot order number.

Figure 5-5: The Edit Series dialog box.

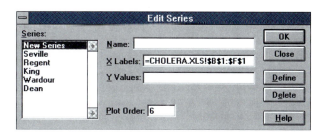

For example, Excel will name the first data series "Series 1," the second data series "Series 2," and so on.

If you want to type in the external reference, or link, formulas yourself, be sure you understand how they work. Refer to the Excel user documentation for more information.

To identify the category names, move the selection cursor to the X Labels text box and enter a link formula that describes the worksheet range holding the category names, or x-axis labels. The easiest way to do this is by selecting the worksheet range that holds the category names, or, in the case of an xy chart, the X data series. If you select the worksheet range B1:F1 in the worksheet named BUDGET, for example, Excel creates the link formula =BUDGET!$B$1:$F$1.

You only need to identify the chart category names, or x-axis labels, for the main chart's first data series and the overlay chart's first data series. In fact, Excel ignores what you enter in the X Labels text box of the second and subsequent data series, unless the chart is an xy chart. In an xy chart, each data series can have its own X labels.

To identify the data-point values that make up the data series, move the selection cursor to the X Labels text box. Then, identify the worksheet range that holds the data point values. The easiest way to do this is by selecting the worksheet range by using the mouse. If you select the range B4:F4 in the worksheet named BUDGET, for example, Excel creates a link formula that describes this range—=BUDGET!$B$4:$F$4. Alternatively, you can also type this link formula yourself.

You can also enter the X Labels and Y Values inputs as named ranges and as array constants. I'm not going to describe here how range names or arrays work, and you don't gain additional functionality by using these methods of identifying category names and data-point values of a data series. If you're still interested, however, refer to the Excel user documentation.

The Plot Order text box allows you to specify where the new data series should be plotted in relation to the existing data series—first, second, third, and so on. Excel adjusts the plot ordering of the existing data series to make room for whatever you choose for the new data series.

Where you've correctly described the data series you want to add, select Define to add the data series and leave the Edit Series dialog box open. Or, select OK to add the data series and close the Edit Series dialog box.

Adding a New Data Series without the Edit Series Command

You don't actually have to use the Edit Series command to add data series to a chart. If you're familiar with the way Excel functions work, you can simply paste or type in a Series function. To paste a series into a chart, select the worksheet range that holds the data-series name and data-point values, copy it with the Edit menu's Copy command, then display the chart's document window and choose the Edit menu's Paste command. Excel pastes the series into the chart.

Typing in a series function is slightly more involved. When you use the Edit Series command, what actually happens is that Excel adds a Series function to the active chart. For example, if you wanted to add, as a chart's third data series, the worksheet range B4:F4 in BUDGET.XLS, and the series name is in cell A4, Excel creates the following series function and adds it to the chart:

=SERIES(Budget!$A$4,Budget!$B$1:$F$1,Budget!$B$4:$F$4,3)

However, you can also just type in this function. The first argument, Budget!$A$4, gives the data-series name, which is exactly what you enter into the Edit Series dialog box's Name text box. The second argument Budget!$B$1:$F$1, gives the category name or X Labels range, which is what you enter in the Edit Series X Labels text box. The third argument, Budget!$B$4:$F$4, gives the data-series range, which is what you enter in the Y Values text box. The fourth argument—3—gives the plot order.

Modifying an Existing Data Series

You can modify an existing data series with the Edit Series command, too. To do this, choose one of the two basic methods available. For most people, the easiest method is to choose the Edit Series command from either the Chart or the shortcut menu. When Excel displays the Edit Series dialog box, select the series you want to change from the Series list box and make the desired changes using the Name, X Labels, Y Values, and Plot Order text boxes. Then, select Define to implement your changes and leave the Edit Series dialog box open. Or, select OK to implement your changes and close the Edit Series dialog box.

If you're comfortable working with the Series function, you can use a second approach for modifying an existing data series. You can click on one of the data markers in the series you want to modify. When you do, Excel displays that data series' Series function on the formula bar. To modify the Series function, just click on the formula bar, edit the Series function as required, and then press Enter or select the Enter command button on the formula bar.

Deleting a Data Series

The easiest way to remove a data series from a chart is to select one of the data series markers and then choose the Edit Clear command. Excel displays the Edit Clear dialog box, which provides two radio buttons: Series and Formats. To remove the selected data series from a chart, mark the Series

Tip!

If you're not comfortable working with the Series function—and most people aren't—don't waste time trying to figure it out. You can accomplish the same things using the Edit Series command.

radio button and select OK. (Mark the Format radio button if you want to remove formatting changes you've previously made to a data marker.)

You can also remove a data series from a chart using the Edit Series command. To do this, choose the Edit Series command, select the series from the Series list box, and then select the Delete command button.

Finally, you can also remove a data series from a chart by removing the appropriate Series function. To do so, click on one of the data markers in the series you want to delete. When Excel displays that data series' Series function on the formula bar, select the entire function, press Delete, and then press Enter or select the Enter command button on the formula bar.

Editing Series in a Three-Dimensional Chart

If you edit data series on a three-dimensional chart, Excel makes some minor changes to the Edit Series dialog box. The Y Values text box is renamed the Y Labels text box, is disabled for entry, and holds the text "Series Name" because Excel uses only the data-series names to label the y-axis in a three-dimensional chart.

Excel also adds a Z Values text box. As you may remember from the discussion in Chapter 3 of the three-dimensional chart types, the z-axis shows the plotted values in a three-dimensional chart in exactly the same way that the y-axis shows the plotted values in a two-dimensional chart. Not surprisingly, then, the Z Values text box works the same way as the Y Values text box for a two-dimensional chart.

Annotating Charts

A chart's messages won't always be clear from looking at the plotted data series. For this reason, you'll want to know about and judiciously use three annotation tools: legends, text boxes, and arrows. In the paragraphs that follow, you'll learn how and when to use each of these handy tools.

As described in Chapter 4, *Drawing*, you can also add text boxes and arrows using Excel's Drawing toolbar. If you've already read Chapter 4, you may want to just skim the sections describing text boxes and arrows.

Legends

Legends, as you already know, identify the plotted data series by visually tying together the data-series name and the color or pattern used in the data markers that plot the series. So, if it isn't clear what you're plotting in a chart, you need either a legend or a labeled data series.

Adding and Removing Chart Legends

To add a legend to a chart, choose the Chart menu's Add Legend command. Or, use the Charting Toolbar's Legend tool. Initially, Excel adds the legend to the right of the plot area, as shown in Figure 5-6.

Excel replaces the Chart menu's Add Legend command with the Delete Legend command if the active chart includes a legend. So, to remove a legend, just choose the Delete Legend

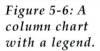

Figure 5-6: A column chart with a legend.

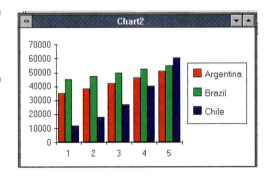

command. Or, select the legend and then choose the Clear command from the Edit menu.

Moving a Legend

Because you've just added the legend, Excel selects the legend so it can be moved easily with the mouse. To indicate the legend is selected, Excel adds selection handles to the legend box's corners and sides. To move the legend with the mouse, click on the legend and then drag it to where you want it positioned.

You can also move a legend with the Legend command. You can select the Legend command from the Format menu or, if the legend is selected, from the shortcut menu. When you select this command, Excel displays the Legend dialog box, as shown in Figure 5-7.

To indicate where you want the legend positioned, you use the Type radio buttons. Simply mark the radio button that corresponds to the legend position you want. Bottom, for example, tells Excel to position the legend beneath the chart plot area.

Changing Legend Borders and Colors

You can change the way Excel draws a border around a legend and the way it colors the interior of the Legend box. To perform either change, use the Patterns command, which you can choose by selecting the Patterns command button on either the

Figure 5-7: The Legend dialog box.

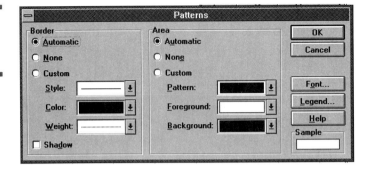

Figure 5-8: The Patterns dialog box.

Legend or Font dialog boxes (see Figures 5-7 and 5-9), or by clicking on the legend to select it, and then choosing the Patterns command from the Format or shortcut menu. Either way, Excel displays the Patterns dialog box shown in Figure 5-8.

To specify how Excel should draw the Legend box's border, use the Border settings. Automatic indicates you want Excel to draw a default Legend box border (which is simply a thin black line). None indicates you don't want a Legend box border. Custom indicates you want to control the appearance of the legend by specifying the line style using the Style drop-down list box, the line color using the Color drop-down list box, and the line thickness using the Weight drop-down list box. The Border settings also let you add a drop shadow to the Legend box simply by marking the Shadow check box.

To specify how Excel should color the interior of the Legend box, you use the Area settings. Automatic indicates you want Excel to color the Legend box white. None indicates you don't want the interior Legend box colored, in which case the box is effectively transparent. Custom indicates you want to control the appearance of the legend by specifying a fill pattern (such as dots) using the Pattern drop-down list box, the color of what is used in the fill pattern (such as dots) using the Foreground drop-down list box, and the color of what is used underneath the fill pattern (such as between the dots) using the Background drop-down list box.

The sample box in the lower-right corner of the Patterns dialog box shows an example Legend box with the border and pattern changes you've made. You can use it to test the effect of your changes without having to leave the Patterns dialog box.

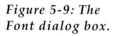

Tip!

The easiest way to select a legend is by clicking a mouse, but it isn't the only way. By pressing any of the four arrows—Up, Down, Left, and Right—Excel alternately selects each of the parts in a chart.

Changing the Legend Text Font

You can change the font of the text Excel writes inside the Legend box. To make this change, use the Font command, which you can choose either by selecting the Font command button on the Legend or Patterns dialog boxes (see Figures 5-7 and 5-8), or by clicking on the legend to select it and then choosing the Font command from the Format or shortcut menu. Either way, Excel displays the Font dialog box shown in Figure 5-9.

To specify which font you want Excel to use, move the selection cursor to the Font text box. Then, either type the font name in the Font text box or select the font from the list box below the text box. Excel identifies True Type fonts by displaying the True Type logo—a pair of capital Ts—in front of the

Figure 5-9: The Font dialog box.

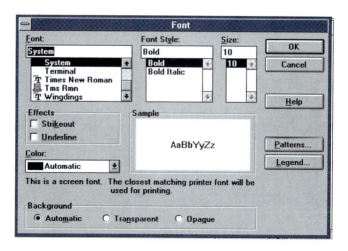

font name in the list box. Excel identifies printer fonts by displaying a tiny picture of printer in front of the font name in the list box. (Near the bottom of the screen, Excel displays a message that describes the compatibility of the selected font and your printer.)

To choose a font style—Regular, Italic, Bold, or Bold Italic—move the selection cursor to the Font Style text box. Then, type the font style name in the Font Style text box, or select the font style from the list box below the text box.

To pick a point size, move the selection cursor to the Size text box. Then, type the desired point size into the text box, or select the point size from the list box. For system and printer fonts, Excel lists the valid fonts in the Size list box. A point is 1/72 of an inch, by the way.

In the unlikely event you want to use any special effects such as strikeouts or underlining, just mark the approach Effect check box—Strikeout or Underline.

To pick the font color—the color of the actual characters—move the selection cursor to the Color drop-down list box, activate the drop down list, and then select the color you want. Initially, font colors are set as automatic, which is the same thing as black. You can, however, change the font color to any of the colors in the document color palette.

To pick the background coloring for fonts—which is the color between the characters such as the interior color of the letter "O"—move the selection cursor to the Background radio buttons set. To use default background coloring, which is usually white, mark the Automatic radio button. To make the font background transparent so you see the Legend box color, mark the Transparent radio button. To show just the Legend box foreground color but no pattern, mark the Opaque radio button.

The sample box in the middle of the Font dialog box shows an example text with the font, style, size, effect, and color changes you've made. You can use it to test the effect of your changes without having to leave the dialog box.

Legends and Chart Design

There are several chart design issues you'll want to consider as you work with legends, including the problem of phantom data markers, redundant data-series identification, text read-ability, legend position, and, finally, chart clutter.

Perhaps the first thing to consider regarding chart legends is whether you even need one. A legend's purpose is to identify the plotted data series by giving their names. So, if it's obvious what a chart plots without giving the data-series names, you don't need a legend. And, if a chart includes data-series names as labels or a data-series axis, you don't need a legend.

You'll want to make sure that your legends don't become phantom data markers. A phantom data marker is simply a graphic object that a chart viewer either mistakenly or subconsciously interprets as an actual graphic object. A legend, because it's a rectangle, may be confused with the rectangles that act as the data markers in bar, column, and combination charts. If you think you don't understand this phantom-data-marker design issue, take another look at Figure 4-13 in the preceding chapter.

Technical Tip

Readability

You also want to keep readability in mind. There's quite a bit of controversy regarding which fonts are and which fonts are not appropriate in data graphics, but the basic argument boils down to one of design versus readability. Professional graphic artists usually say you should use sans serif fonts like Helvetica and Ariel because they're cleaner and more eye-appealing. Data analysts usually say you should use serif fonts like Times Roman and Times New Roman because they've been proven easier to read.

Sans serif simply means "without serif." Serifs are the little cross strokes appearing on characters. So, sans serif fonts don't have the little cross-strokes, and serif fonts do. This book, for example, is written using a serif font because the serif makes it easier for your eyes to move from character to character. If you're confused about sans serif versus serif, compare the letters on the following two lines. The first line, which is the same as the font used for this book, is a serif font. The second line is a sans serif font.

| Serif: | A | b | C | D | E | f | g |
| Sans serif: | A | b | C | D | E | f | g |

One other thing to consider regarding text readability is the text color in relation to the background color. In general, you want maximum contrast between these two colors. Black on white is easiest to read, which is one of the reasons that books like this one use black ink and white paper. Other contrasting color combinations also work well, however, such as dark blue on yellow. You can put light colors on a dark background, too—and sometimes you must, as in the case of a 35mm slide. However, studies show that, in general, dark text on a light background is more legible than light text on a dark background.

Legend position needs to be considered, too. Here's the basic problem. In most cases, a legend isn't a very convenient way to identify the plotted data series. The reason is that chart viewers are required to look between the chart plot area and the Legend box. The greater the distance between the legend and the plot area, of course, the more work for the viewer in using the legend. So, you'll usually want to position a legend as close to the plot area as possible—maybe even inside the plot area.

One final point concerning legends: in general, your legends should be as visually simple as possible to reduce chart clutter. For this reason, you probably want to consider removing all nonessential parts of a legend. For example, you may want to remove the legend box border because it adds no information. And, for the same reason, you may want to avoid special effects, like the drop shadow or unique coloring.

Text Boxes

You already know about text boxes if you read Chapter 4. Text boxes are simply boxes that hold text. You use them to add notes and comments to a chart. While you need to be careful you don't clutter a chart with extraneous text, text boxes do provide a helpful way to annotate the data plotted in a chart.

Adding a Text Box

As mentioned in Chapter 4, one way to add a text box is with the Text Box command on the Drawing toolbar. Using the Drawing toolbar's Text Box tool, you can add text boxes to charts embedded in worksheets and to charts displayed in their own document windows. Another way to add a text box to a chart displayed in its own document window, however, is to just type whatever text you want to appear on the chart and press Enter. For example, if you type the phrase "This is a text

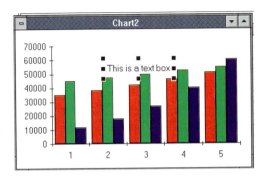

*Figure 5-10: A
text box. This
text box has
selection han-
dles on its
corners and sides.*

box" and press Enter, Excel adds a text box like the one shown in Figure 5-10.

After you add a text box, Excel selects it so you can move or resize it.

To edit the text in a text box, select the text box by clicking on it. When a text box is selected, Excel displays its text on the formula bar. To change the text, click the formula bar and then edit the text as necessary. Press Enter or click on the formula bar's Enter command button when you complete your editing.

Excel attempts to break up your text in lines that fit neatly into the box size you choose. You can control where your text is broken into lines, however. To break text into lines in a chart document window, press Alt-Enter at the point you want one line to end and Excel to advance to the next line. To break text into lines in a text box in a worksheet, press Enter.

Technical Tip

Linking Text

You don't have to enter text into a text box. You can also link the text in a text box to a cell on a work-sheet using an external reference. In this case, what the text box displays is whatever the referenced worksheet cell displays. To create a text- box-to-worksheet-cell link, type an equals sign, click on the cell to which the text box should be linked, and press Enter. Excel creates a link formula for the text box so it displays whatever the linked-to worksheet cell displays. You can also type the link formula yourself. For example, to retrieve the text in cell A1 in the worksheet named BUDGET and use it in a text box, you type =BUDGET!$A$1. (If you want more information about how link formulas work, refer to the Excel user documentation.)

There are a couple of things you should know, however, if you use external references. While normally you can format the text in a text box in any way you like, you can't format text that is retrieved using a link. The reason for this is that Excel uses the same text formatting as the worksheet cell.

Another issue to consider regarding linked text is this: the Spelling command, which appears on the Options and Chart menus, checks the text in the active document window. Therefore, if you retrieve text into a chart using a link, you don't actually check the spelling of the linked text by checking the spelling of the text in the chart document window. To verify the spelling of linked text, you need to check the spelling of the worksheet document window containing the text retrieved through the link. (Chapter 6 describes how you use the Spelling command to verify the spelling of all chart text.)

Removing Text Boxes

To remove a text box from a chart or worksheet, select it using the mouse or arrow keys. Then, choose the Edit menu's Clear command or press the Delete key. You can also remove text boxes by selecting the text box so it's contents are displayed on the formula bar, clicking on the formula bar, selecting the contents of the formula bar, and then pressing the delete key.

Moving and Resizing Text Boxes

You can move a text box with either the mouse or the Format menu's Move command. To move a text box with the mouse, click on the text box and then drag it. To move a text box with the Format menu's Move command, select it if it isn't already selected, choose the Move command, and then use the arrow keys to move the box. To move a text box in smaller increments, hold down the Ctrl key while you press the arrow keys.

You can resize a text with either the mouse or the Format menu's Size command. To change the dimensions of a text box using the mouse, click on a selection handle and then drag it in the direction you want the text box's dimension to change. To change the dimensions of a text box using the Format menu's Size command, select the text box, choose the Size command, and then use the Left and Right Arrow keys to move the right edge of the box and the Up and Down Arrow keys to move the top edge of the box. To resize the text box with smaller changes, hold down the Ctrl key while you press the arrow keys.

Changing Text Box Fonts

Just as you can control the font characteristics of legend text, you can also control the font characteristics of text box text. To change the characteristics of text box text such as font, style, and point size, first select the text box by clicking on it with

Tip!

Although it's the easiest way to select a text box, you don't have to use the mouse. You can also use the arrow keys. By pressing any of the four arrows—Up, Down, Left, and Right—you can alternately select each of the parts in a chart.

the mouse. Then, choose the Font command. You can choose the Font command from the Format or shortcut menu. (The Font command button, which appears on several dialog boxes, also chooses the Font command.)

No matter how you choose the Font command, when you do, Excel displays the Font dialog box, which closely resembles the one shown earlier in the chapter in Figure 5-9. Using the Font dialog box, you can choose a font, font style, and point size; use special effects; and control text color. The Font dialog box works the same way for text boxes as it does for legend text. Therefore, if you have questions about how to use the Font dialog box to change text box text, refer to the earlier discussion of changing legend text.

Changing the Text Box Border and Color

You can also change the way Excel draws a border around a text box and the way it colors the interior of the text box. To perform either change, select the text box and then choose the Patterns command from the Format or shortcut menu. (The Patterns command button, which appears on several dialog boxes also chooses the Patterns command.)

Excel displays a Patterns dialog box, which closely resembles the one shown earlier in Figure 5-8. To specify how Excel should draw the legend box's border, use the Border settings. To specify how Excel should color the interior of the legend box, use the Area settings. I described earlier how these settings work in the case of a legend box. They work the same way for a text box. If you have questions, refer to the earlier chapter section titled "Changing Legend Borders and Colors."

Changing Text Alignment and Orientation

You can change the way Excel aligns text and orients text in a text box. To make these changes, select the text box and then choose the Text command from the Format or shortcut menu.

(The Text command button, which appears on several dialog boxes, also chooses the Text command.) When you choose the Text command, Excel displays a Text dialog box like the one shown in Figure 5-11.

The Text Alignment settings control how Excel horizontally and vertically aligns text in a text box. By default, Excel aligns text so it is centered both horizontally and vertically. You can change the horizontal alignment, however, so text is aligned to the left edge of the box, aligned to the right edge of the box, or justified. (When text is horizontally justified, Excel spaces the letters so each line of text starts at the left edge of the box and ends at the right edge of the box.)

You can also change the vertical alignment of the text in text boxes. The Top setting aligns text to the top edge of the box. The Bottom setting aligns text to the bottom edge of the box. The Justify setting spaces the lines of text so the first line is flush with the top edge of the box and the last line is flush with the bottom edge of the box.

The Orientation settings show the four ways of presenting text. The default left-to-right orientation is the easiest to read, so you'll almost always want to use it. You have the choice, however, of choosing another orientation. To change the orientation, just click the command button that shows text arranged the way you want your text box text arranged.

Figure 5-11: The Text dialog box.

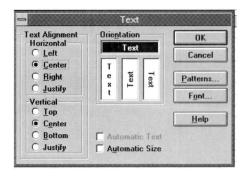

You'll also notice that there are two check boxes on the Text dialog box: Automatic Text and Automatic Size. The Automatic Text check box, if marked, tells Excel to restore the default text it creates for attached text boxes. (I'll talk about attached text boxes next.) The Automatic Size check box, if marked, tells Excel to adjust the size of the text box so your text fits in the box.

Attaching Text Boxes

You can attach text boxes to parts of a chart. There are a couple of reasons for doing this. One is that Excel then moves the text box if the part of the chart to which the text box is attached moves. The other reason for attaching text boxes to a part of a chart is that Excel will provide default text for some attached text boxes if you mark the Automatic Text check box on the Text dialog box (see Figure 5-11).

To attach a text box to a part of a chart, first select the text box by clicking on it. Then, choose the Attach Text command from the Chart menu. Excel displays the Attach Chart dialog box, shown in Figure 5-12.

To indicate to which part of a chart the selected text box should be attached, mark one of the dialog box radio buttons: Chart Title, Value (Y) Axis, Category (X) Axis, Series and Data

Figure 5-12: The Attach Chart dialog box. Mark one of the dialog box radio buttons to identify where on the chart the text box should be attached.

Point, Overlay Value (Y) Axis, or Overlay Category (X) Axis. If you choose to attach a text box to a specific data point (indicated when you mark the Series and Data Point radio button), you'll also need to identify the data point by entering the number of the series and the data point in the text boxes provided. With area charts, you can't attach a text box to a specific data point, so you only have to enter a series number.

If the active chart is three-dimensional, Excel changes the name of the Values (Y) Axis to Values (Z) Axis and provides another radio button, Series (Y) Axis, which you use to attach text to the data series axis. If you have questions about the axes used for three-dimensional chart types, refer to Chapter 3.

Arrows

Arrows represent another chart annotation tool available in Excel. You can use arrows to point out important data points or relationships. You can also use arrows to visually connect the information in a text box to some part of the chart.

Adding Arrows

While you can add arrows to Excel charts using the Drawing toolbar, Excel also provides a command, Add Arrow, which appears on the Chart menu. To use the Add Arrow command, simply select it. Excel then adds an arrow to the chart window and selects it so you can move it. Figure 5-13 shows a chart window that has just had an arrow added to it.

You'll need to move and resize the arrow so it looks exactly the way you want. To move the arrow with the mouse, point to the arrow, and drag it in the direction it should be moved in. To change the size of the arrow with the mouse, point the selection handle at the end you want to shorten or lengthen, and drag it in the direction you want it to go.

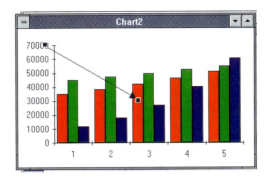

Figure 5-13: A chart window with an arrow added to it. Excel adds arrows in the position and of the size shown here.

You can also move and resize an arrow using the Format menu's Move and Resize commands. To move an arrow with the Move command, select the arrow, choose the command, and then use the arrow keys. To resize an arrow with the Size command, select the arrow, choose the command, and then use the arrow keys to move the arrow head, thereby changing the arrow size. To move or resize the arrow in smaller increments, you can hold down the Ctrl key while you press the arrow keys.

To remove an arrow from a chart, select the arrow. Then, press the Del key, or select the Clear command from the Edit or shortcut menu. Or, choose the Delete Arrow command from the Chart menu. (The Delete Arrow command replaces the Add Arrow command if an arrow is selected.)

Changing Arrow Appearance

You can change the way arrows look by changing the arrow shaft, or line, and the arrow head. To make either change, you first need to select the Arrow. Then, choose the Patterns command from the Format menu or the shortcut menu. Excel displays the Patterns dialog box shown in Figure 5-14 on the following page.

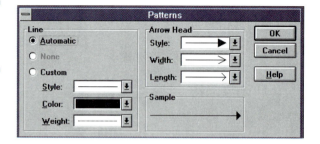

To change the way the arrow shaft looks, use the Line settings. Mark the Automatic radio button if you want Excel to use the default Arrow-Shaft setting: a thin, solid, black line. Mark the None radio button if you don't want Excel to draw arrows with shafts. Mark the Custom radio button if you want to specifically control the style, color, and weight of the arrow shaft. If you have questions about any of these settings, just activate the drop-down list boxes. They show the available choices.

To change the way the arrow head looks, of course, you use the Arrow Head settings: Style, Width, and Length. Again, the easiest way to understand the different arrow head settings is just to activate the three drop-down list boxes, because the list boxes show the alternate style, width, and length settings.

Note, too, that in the lower-right corner of the Patterns dialog box, there is a sample box that shows how an arrow looks with the current line and arrow head settings.

Annotation and Chart Design

As you annotate your charts with such things as text boxes and arrows, there are a couple of design issues you'll want to keep in mind: the importance of readability and the problem of phantom data markers.

First and foremost, of course, you'll want to make the text in your text boxes easy to read. Ironically, though, many of the text formatting options actually reduce readability. As noted in the earlier discussion of the legend text, while there is controversy regarding appropriate fonts for presentation graphics, I suggest serif fonts for the sake of readability. Avoid special effects—particularly underlining—because they reduce readability. Use text and background color combinations that provide for maximum contrast—black on white, for example. And shy away from text orientation other than the standard left-to-right rows of characters.

Both text boxes and arrows can become phantom data markers—graphic objects that viewers either mistakenly or subconsciously interpret as data markers—so you'll want to watch out for this problem. Text boxes most easily become phantom data markers on column and bar charts because they both use rectangular data markers—the same shape as text boxes. Arrows most easily become phantom data markers on line charts because the arrow can, in effect, visually extend a plotted line.

Changing Other Graphic Objects

You can also change the appearance of other graphic objects created using the Drawing tools described in Chapter 4. To do this, you select the graphic object—the line, rectangle, circle, or whatever—and then choose the Patterns command from either the regular menu bar's Format menu or from the shortcut menu. Excel displays a Patterns dialog box very similar in appearance and operation to the Patterns dialog box shown in Figure 5-8. You then make changes to such things as the object border and color using this dialog box.

Adding and Changing Axes

Excel allows you to customize chart axes to better quantify a chart's data markers and to better identify both the categories and series. In the next few paragraphs, you'll learn how to customize axes easily and quickly.

Adding and Removing Axes

You add and remove axes from charts using the Axes command, which appears on both the Chart menu and the shortcut menu. Using the command is simple. When you choose the command, Excel displays a dialog box that lists check boxes for each of the axes you can display on a chart. Figure 5-15, for example, shows the Axes dialog box that Excel displays if the chart is a two-dimensional chart with just a main chart. To add a category axis, you mark the Category (X) Axis check box. To add a value axis, you mark the Value (Y) Axis check box. To remove an axis, of course, you just unmark its check box. Or, you can remove an axis by selecting it and then choosing the Clear command from the Edit or shortcut menu.

If the active chart includes both a main chart and an overlay chart, the Axes dialog box also include two sets of check boxes: one for the main chart and one for the overlay chart. If the active chart uses a three-dimensional plot area so that it has a series axes, too, the Axes dialog box also includes a check box for the Series Axis.

Changing a Category Axis

You can change the axis scale settings for a chart's category axis, thereby controlling where the value axis crosses the category axis, how the category axis is labeled, and where category-axis tick marks are located. To make these changes to a

Figure 5-15: The Axes dialog box.

category axis, first select the axis by clicking on it with the mouse. Then, choose the Scale command from the Format menu or the shortcut menu. Either way, Excel displays an Axis Scale dialog box like the one shown in Figure 5-16.

Tip!

Although it's the easiest way to select an axis, you don't have to use the mouse. You can also use the arrow keys. By pressing any of the four arrows—Up, Down, Left, and Right—You can alternately select each of the parts in a chart.

To control which value, or y, axis should cross the category axis, move the selection cursor to the Value (Y) Axis Crosses At Category Number text box. Then, enter the category number before which the value axis should cross the category axis. For example, if you want the value axis to appear at the left end of the category axis, before the first category, enter a 1.

You can't control where the value axis crosses the category axis for three-dimensional charts. The value axis must appear at the left end of the category axis, before the first category.

To control how Excel labels categories, move the selection cursor to the Number Of Categories Between Tick Labels text box. Then, enter a 1 if every category should be labeled with a category name; a 2 if every other category should be labeled with a category name; a 3 if every third category should be labeled with a category name; and so on. As long as you have room, it usually makes for easier viewing if you label each category.

To specify how many categories Excel should draw between a pair of category-axis tick marks, move the selection cursor to

Figure 5-16: The Category (X) Axis Scale dialog box.

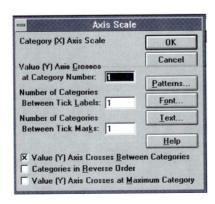

the Number Of Categories Between Tick Marks text box. Then, enter an appropriate value: 1 if Excel should draw tick marks between each category's data points, 2 if Excel should draw tick marks between every second category's data points, and so on.

The Value (Y) Axis Crosses Between Categories check box controls where Excel draws the value axis: at the edge of the category, or through the middle of the category specified in the Value Axis Crosses At Category Number, or through the middle of the first category. You'll want Excel to draw the value axis at the edge of a category rather than through it to maximize the legibility of the value-axis scale. (You can control value-axis placement for three-dimensional area and line charts, too, using these settings. For a three-dimensional chart, Excel changes the check box name to Value (Z) Axis Crosses Between Categories, however, since the value axis is called the Z axis on a three-dimensional chart.)

The Categories In Reverse Order check box, if marked, causes Excel to flip-flop the left-to-right order of the categories and the data points within a category. This check box does not, however, change the plot order of the data series.

Finally, the Value (Y) Axis Crosses At Maximum Category check box overrides the Value (Y) Axis Crosses At Category Number text box. If this check box is marked, Excel draws the value axis after the category with the largest data-point values. This category axis scale setting isn't available for three-dimensional chart types.

The Patterns, Text, and Font command buttons let you change category-axis patterns, text orientation, and text-font specifications. A little later in this chapter section, I'll describe exactly how you do this.

Changing a Value Axis

You can change the axis scale settings for a chart's value axis, too, including specifying exactly how the value axis should be calibrated. To make these changes to a category axis, first select the value axis by clicking on it with the mouse. Then, choose the Scale command from the Format menu or the shortcut menu. Either way, Excel displays an Axis Scale dialog box like the one shown in Figure 5-17.

The Minimum check and text boxes control the smallest value shown on the value axis. If you mark the Auto Minimum check box, Excel enters a minimum value for you in the Minimum text box. Excel creates a minimum value by rounding the smallest data-point value down to the nearest major axis scaling unit—usually zero.

The Maximum check and text boxes control the largest value shown on the value axis. If you mark the Auto Maximum check box, Excel enters a maximum value for you in the Maximum text box. Excel creates a maximum value by rounding the largest data-point value up to the nearest major axis scaling unit.

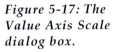

Figure 5-17: The Value Axis Scale dialog box.

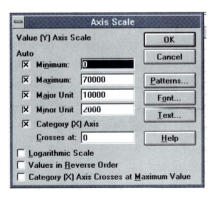

The Major Unit check and text boxes control the calibration of the value axis into its major units of measurement. If you mark the Auto Major Unit check box, Excel enters a major scaling increment that calibrates the value axis into between five and 10 increments. For major scaling increments, Excel attempts to use easy-to-factor numbers, such as 1, 2, 50, 100, and so on.

The Minor Unit check and text boxes control the calibration of the value axis into its minor units of measurement. If you mark the Auto Minor Unit check box, Excel enters a minor scaling increment that splits each major scaling increment into five minor scaling increments. So, if the major scaling increment is 10, the minor scaling increment is 2.

The Category (X) Axis Crosses At check and text box control where on the value axis the category axis crosses or connects. If you mark the Auto check box, the category axis crosses the value axis at the value-axis minimum.

In a case where you're scaling the vertical value axis of an xy chart, this check and text box combination, renamed Value (Y) Crosses At, controls where the y-axis crosses the x-axis. In the case of three-dimensional charts with three-dimensional plot areas, this check and text box combination, renamed Floor (XY Plane) Crosses At, controls where the plot-area floor crosses the value axis (z-axis). Because radar charts don't use a two-dimensional or three-dimensional plot area, this check and text box combination isn't available for radar charts.

The Logarithmic Scale check box lets you turn on and off logarithmic scaling of the value axis. Chapter 2 describes why you use logarithmic scaling; refer to it if you have questions.

The Values In Reverse Order check box, if marked, causes Excel to reverse the values on the value axis so the minimum appears at the top of the value axis and the maximum appears at the bottom of the value axis. (For xy scatter charts, this check box, renamed the Categories In Reverse Order check box, reverses the x-axis scale. The check box is not available for radar charts, however.)

Finally, the Category (X) Axis Crosses At Maximum Value check box overrides Category (X) Axis Crosses At check and text boxes, by specifying that Excel draw the category axis above the largest data-point value. On xy charts, the check box name changes to Value (Y) Axis Crosses At Maximum Category, but it works the same way. This value-axis scale setting isn't available for three-dimensional chart types, however. If the active chart is a 3D chart, Excel doesn't show the Category (X) Axis Crosses At Maximum Value check box. In its place, it shows a Floor (XY Plane) Crosses At Minimum Value check box, which overrides the Floor (XY Plane) Crosses At value.

The Patterns, Text, and Font command buttons let you change value-axis patterns, text font, and text-orientation specifications. A little later in this chapter section, I'll describe exactly how you do this.

Changing the Series Axis in a Three-Dimensional Chart

You can also make some changes to the series axis on a chart with a three-dimensional plot area. To modify a series axis, you first select the axis by clicking on it with the mouse. Then, you choose the Axis Scale command from the Format menu or the shortcut menu. Either way, Excel displays an Axis Scale dialog box like the one shown in Figure 5-18.

The Number Of Series Between Tick Labels text box lets you control which data-series are labeled with data series names. Enter a 1 if you want Excel to label every data series; a number greater than 1 if you want Excel to label alternate series. For example, enter a 2 if you want Excel to label every second series; a 3 if you want Excel to label every third series, and so on.

*Figure 5-18: The
Series Axis Scale
dialog box.*

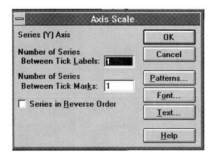

The Number Of Series Between Tick Marks text box works like
the similarly entitled text boxes on the other Axis Scale dialog
boxes. It simply specifies how often Excel should draw tick
marks on the series axis. A 1 indicates that Excel should draw
a tick mark after each data series. A 2 indicates that Excel
should draw a tick mark after every second data series. A 3
indicates that Excel should draw a tick mark after every third
data series.

Finally, the Series In Reverse Order check box just flip-flops
the order in which data series are plotted in the three-dimensional area. With this check box marked, for example, Excel
draws the first data series last so that it is further back in the
plot area background, and the last data series first so that it is
in the foreground.

The Patterns, Font, and Text Orientation command buttons let
you change series-axis patterns, text font, and text-orientation
specifications. In the next section, I'll describe exactly how you
do this.

Changing Scale Patterns,
Font, and Text Orientation Settings

As with other elements of a chart, Excel also lets you change a
scale's patterns, the font used for the scale's labels, and the
orientation of the text used for the scale's labels. To make one

or more of these changes, first select the axis you want to change. Then, choose the Patterns command from either the Format menu or the shortcuts menu. You can also choose the Patterns command by selecting the Patterns command button on one of the Axis Scale dialog boxes shown in Figures 5-16, 5-17, or 5-18. Once you choose the Patterns dialog box, Excel displays a Patterns dialog box like the one shown in Figure 5-19.

To change the way the axis-scale line looks, use the Axis settings. Mark the Automatic radio button if you want Excel to use the default Axis-Scale Line setting: a thin, solid, black line. Mark the None radio button if you don't want Excel to draw an axis scale line. Mark the Custom radio button if you want to control the style, color, and weight of the axis scale line. If you have questions about any of these settings, just activate the drop-down list boxes. They show the available choices.

In the lower-right corner of the Patterns dialog box, there's a sample box that shows an example of the axis scale line. Unfortunately, the sample doesn't show tick marks and labels.

To change the way the major and minor tick marks look, use the Tick Mark Type Major and Tick Mark Type Minor settings. Mark None if you don't want a tick mark; Mark Inside if you

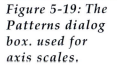

Figure 5-19: The Patterns dialog box. used for axis scales.

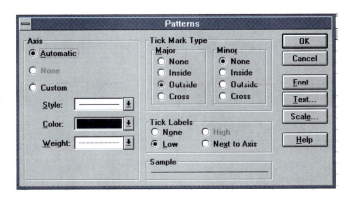

want tick marks to show as marks that extend perpendicularly into the plot area; Mark Outside if you want tick marks to extend perpendicularly away from the plot area; or Mark Cross if you want tick marks to intersect the axis scale line.

To control if and where Excel positions tick mark-labels, use the Tick Labels settings. Mark None if you don't want Excel to add tick-mark labels. Mark Low if you want Excel to add tick-mark labels at the low end of the axis. Mark High if you want Excel to add tick-mark labels at the high end of the axis. Finally, mark Next to Axis if you want Excel To add tick-mark labels next to the axis.

Let me also make some minor points related to the tick labels. As with all chart text, you should keep the issue of readability in mind as you make any changes to the tick labels that support value, category, and series axes. For example, don't use text formatting options, like underlining, that reduce readability. Stick with serif fonts. Use text and background color combinations, like black on white, that provide for maximum contrast. And shy away from text orientation other than the standard left-to-right rows of characters.

Technical Tip

Axis Changes and Chart Design

Perhaps the most important thing you need to consider is the problem of misleading value-axis scaling. In fact, there are two potential problems related to value-axis scaling. The first scaling problem is this: because the dominant visual elements of a graph are the plotted data series, the calibration of the y-axis scaling is easy to overlook. For example, data-point values that are plotted as tall bars are interpreted as large values. Data-point values that are plotted as short bars are interpreted as small values. And striking differences in bar height are interpreted as significant. The problem with these first impressions is that they're right only if the y-axis scaling uses appropriate minimum, maximum, major, and minor unit settings. So, if you use a minimum setting of 0 and a maximum setting of, say, a billion, even large data-point values appear small. And if you use very small increments and the smallest possible range between the minimum and maximum, minuscule differences between data points appear monstrous. The solution to this problem, of course, is to use common sense in setting your value axis scaling rather than relying strictly on the characteristics of your data.

A second scaling problem occurs when you're viewing two or more charts, and the charts plot related data, such as department costs or sales and profits. To make two charts readily comparable, you must use the same value-axis scale: the same minimum setting, the same maximum setting, and the same major and minor unit settings. Otherwise, it becomes needlessly difficult for people reading the graph to compare and contrast plotted data. For example, to compare a bar in a first chart that's 1-inch tall and calibrated in $1,000 increments to a bar in a second chart that's 2-inches tall and calibrated in $250 increments, you'll need both a ruler and a calculator.

Another thing you may want to consider is using your value axes to communicate additional data rather than using them simply to calibrate your data markers. For example, if you were plotting the fat content in servings of various foods, you might set the value-axis maximum to the adult maximum daily-fat allowance recommended by, say, the U.S. Food and Drug Administration. In this way, not only would your value scale calibrate the fat content of various foods, it would also compare the plotted data point values to a well-known dietary standard.

Adding and Customizing Gridlines

You can add gridlines to any Excel chart type except the two- and three-dimensional pie charts. In addition, you can customize the gridlines Excel draws by specifying exactly what you want the lines to look like. The steps for performing either change are easy and straightforward.

Adding and Removing Gridlines

To add gridlines to a chart, for example, select the Gridlines command from the Chart menu. When you do, Excel displays the Gridlines dialog box, as shown in Figure 5-20.

To add gridlines that extend perpendicularly from the category axis, use the Category (X) Axis check boxes. Mark the Major Gridlines check box if you want gridlines drawn from the major tick marks of the category axis. Mark the Minor Gridlines check box if you want gridlines drawn from the minor tick marks of the category axis. Or, if you want to remove category-axis gridlines, just unmark the appropriate check box.

Figure 5-20: The Gridlines dialog box.

In a similar fashion, to add gridlines that extend perpendicularly from the value axis, use the Value (Y) Axis check boxes. Mark the Major Gridlines check box if you want gridlines drawn from the major tick marks of the value axis. Mark the Minor Gridlines check box if you want gridlines drawn from the minor tick marks of the value axis. Again, if you want to remove value-axis gridlines, just unmark the appropriate check box.

For charts with three-dimensional plot areas, Excel displays a third set of check boxes for specifying whether the series axis should have gridlines.

Customizing Gridlines

You can change the style, color, and weight of the lines you use to create gridlines by selecting the gridlines you want to change (usually with the mouse) and then choosing the Patterns command from the Format menu or the shortcut menu. When you choose the Patterns command, Excel displays the Patterns dialog box, as shown in Figure 5-21.

To change the way the gridlines looks, use the Line settings, of course. Mark the Automatic radio button if you want Excel to use the default Gridlines setting: a thin, solid, black line. Or, mark the Custom radio button if you want to specifically control the style, color, and weight of the gridlines.

Tip!

Although it's the easiest way to select gridlines, you don't have to use the mouse. You can also use the arrow keys. By pressing any of the four arrows—Up, Down, Left, and Right—you alternately select each of the parts in a chart.

Figure 5-21: The gridlines Patterns dialog box.

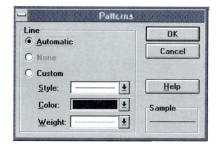

Gridlines and Chart Design

The purpose of gridlines is to make it easier to quantify plotted data-point values. This purpose, however, brings up a couple of interesting design issues. The first is whether gridlines are even needed to quantify data point values. Clearly, in many cases, they aren't, because it's easy enough to quantify data-point values using the value axis or value axes. If your gridlines don't help viewers better understand the data, they merely clutter the chart, distract the viewer, and reduce the chart's readability.

There's also a related point worth discussing. Gridlines, because they are lines, can fairly easily hide data plotted in line charts. Therefore, if you do add gridlines to a line chart, you need to verify that your gridlines don't hide or camouflage the plotted data. The easiest way to ensure that this does not happen is to use very thin, different-colored gridlines so that the line chart's lines stand out. For example, if you use solid, medium-weight black lines for the line chart's lines, you could use dashed, thin, gray lines for the gridlines.

Changing Data Markers

If you've read this far, you won't be surprised to find that Excel also lets you change the appearance of some charts' data markers. In fact, you can change the data markers for all charts (except the surface chart types) using techniques similar to those already described for other parts of a chart. In this final chapter section, I'll describe how you can change the lines, colors, and shapes used for data markers. In addition, I'll describe how you can use graphical images for data markers.

Tip!

You can also use the arrow keys to select a data series' data markers. By pressing any of the four arrows—Up, Down, Left, and Right—you alternately select each of the graphical elements in a chart.

Changing Data Markers in Two-Dimensional Line, XY, and Radar Charts

In two-dimensional line, xy, and radar charts, you can change both the line and the symbols used to show the actual data points. To make either change, first select the data-series data markers you want to change by clicking on the series with the mouse. Or, if you want to change only a single data point's data markers, hold down the Ctrl key and click on the data point's data markers.

Then, to change the selected data markers, you choose the Patterns command from the Format or shortcut menu. Excel displays the Patterns dialog box like the one shown in Figure 5-22.

The Line settings, of course, control the appearance of the line that connects the data-marker symbols. If you want Excel to automatically format the lines—which usually means the lines are solid, thin, and black—mark the Automatic radio button. If you don't want lines between the data-marker symbols, mark the None radio button. If you want to format the lines, mark the Custom radio button. Then, use the Style, Color, and Weight drop-down list boxes to specify how you want the line to look. The easiest way to see what the various style, color, and weight settings do is to select various options and then

Figure 5-22: The Patterns dialog box. This dialog box can be used to change data markers for two-dimensional line, xy, and radar charts.

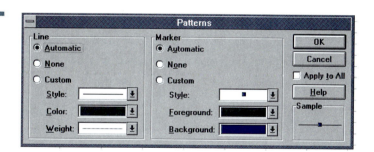

look at the Sample picture box in the lower-right corner of the dialog box.

The Marker settings control the appearance of the data-point markers. Mark the Automatic radio button if you want Excel to use the default data-point symbols—small squares. Mark the None radio button if you don't want Excel to use data-marker symbols. Or, mark the Custom radio button to control the appearance of the data markers. Then, use the Style, Foreground Color, and Background Color drop-down list boxes to specify the data marker appearance. Again, the easiest way to see how the Style, Foreground Color, and Background Color settings affect data markers is to look at the Sample picture box in the lower-right corner of the dialog box.

The Patterns dialog box, shown in Figure 5-22, provides one other useful tool. If you want Excel to apply the specified line and marker settings to all the data markers in all the charts' series, you can mark the Apply To All check box. In the case of a combination chart, however, the Apply To All check box only applies the pattern settings to the data series in the chart with the selected data series. In other words, if you select a data series in the main chart, make patterns changes, and then mark the Apply To All check box, Excel modifies all the data series in the main chart but not the data series in the overlay chart.

Changing Data Markers in Area, Bar, Column, Pie, and Three-Dimensional Line Charts

You can change both the line used to draw a border around the data markers in area, bar, column, pie, and three-dimensional line charts as well as the interior shape, or area. To make either change, first select the data series data markers you want to change by clicking on the series with the mouse. Or, if you want to change only an individual data marker,

Tip!

hold down the Ctrl key and click on the data point's data markers.

To change the selected data markers, you next choose the Patterns command from the Format or shortcut menu. Excel displays the Patterns dialog box like the one shown in Figure 5-23.

The Border settings, of course, control the appearance of the line that Excel draws around the data marker. To use the default Border setting—a solid, thin, black line—mark the Automatic radio button. If you don't want borders drawn around the data markers, mark the None radio button. Or, if you want to format the lines, mark the Custom radio button. Then, use the Style, Color, and Weight drop-down list boxes to specify how you want the border to look. The easiest way to see what these settings do is to select different setting options and then look at the Sample picture box in the lower-right corner of the dialog box.

The Area settings control the interior data marker pattern and color. Mark the Automatic radio button if you want Excel to use the default pattern and color scheme: solid colors for each data series starting with the third color in the Excel color palette—red. Mark the None radio button if you want to use transparent rather than colored data markers. Or, mark the

Figure 5-23: The Patterns dialog box. This dialog box can be used to change data markers for area, bar, column, pie, and three-dimensional line charts.

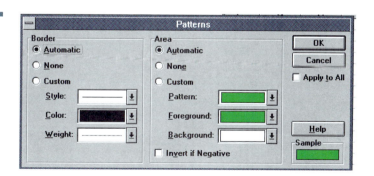

Custom radio button to control the appearance of the data-marker interior. The Patterns drop-down list box lists the available interior patterns such as solid, dots, stripes, and so on. The Foreground, which lists the 16 colors in the document color palette, controls the colors of the dots or stripes used to create the pattern. The Background, which also lists the 16 colors in the document color palette, controls the colors underneath and between the dots or stripes, or whatever was used to create the pattern. If you have questions about how the Pattern, Foreground Color, and Background Color settings affect the data-marker interior, use the Sample picture box in the lower-right corner of the dialog box to experiment.

The Patterns dialog box in Figure 5-23 also provides two check boxes for controlling data-marker formatting. The Invert If Negative check box, which is also one of the Patterns settings, swaps the Foreground and Background Color settings if the plotted value is a negative number. If you want Excel to apply the specified border and area settings to all the data markers in all the main chart's or overlay chart's series, you can mark the Apply To All check box.

Using Pictures as Data Markers

You can use graphical images, or pictures, as data markers, too. To do this, first copy the image you want to use to the Windows Clipboard. Usually, you do this by selecting the image you want to use and then choosing the Copy command from the Edit menu. Next, you display the Excel chart in which you want to use a picture data marker and select the data marker you want to replace. Then, you choose the Edit menu's Paste command . Figure 5-24 shows a graphical image as a data marker.

Usually, you'll use picture data markers in bar and column charts. You can also use picture data markers in line, radar,

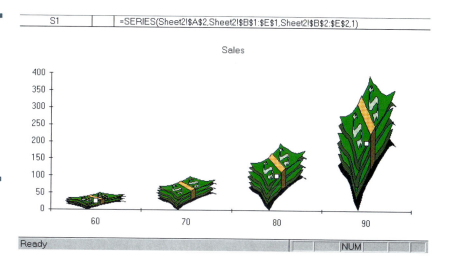

Figure 5-24: A picture column chart. This shows a picture column chart with a stack of dollar bills used as the data marker.

and xy charts, however. For these chart types, the picture is used for the symbol data markers.

If you use picture data markers in a chart, Excel uses a miniature version of the picture in your chart legend, if there is one.

To control how Excel uses and manipulates picture data markers, select one of the picture data markers with the mouse and then choose the Patterns command from either the Format or shortcut menu. Excel then displays the Patterns dialog box shown in Figure 5-25.

To control how Excel changes pictures to show changing data-point values, use the Picture Format radio buttons. Mark the Stretch radio button to show changes in the data-point values by stretching and shrinking the picture. Mark the Stack radio button to show changes in data-point values by stacking equal-sized pictures. Or, mark the Stack And Scale radio button to show changes by stacking pictures and, at the same time, to specify how many units each picture represents, using the Units/Picture text box.

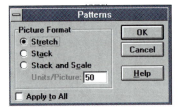

Figure 5-25: The picture-data-marker Patterns dialog box.

If you want Excel to use the picture and the picture-format settings for all the data series in the main chart or overlay chart, you can just mark the Apply To All check box.

Data Markers and Chart Design

Several chart design issues are raised when you modify the characteristics of data markers, as described in the preceding pages. Probably the most important is the challenge of using color correctly. Unfortunately, there is a fundamental problem with using color in charts: color neither identifies the data nor describes the data. This may sound like an odd criticism. After all, color is used in all sorts of other graphic designs: slick corporate brochures, catchy advertisements, fine art, and so on. Why shouldn't it be used in a chart?

The answer is simply that charts are not slick corporate brochures, catchy advertisements, or fine art. They are data-comparison tools. And, unfortunately, when you use color (particularly when you go wild with color), you usually don't do anything to make the data more understandable or comparable. In fact, you may even make the data less understandable and less comparable.

In most cases, color doesn't, by itself, identify data series or data points. And color doesn't generally show order or magnitude because colors have no numeric value.

You can sometimes show order or magnitude with achromatic color schemes (like white, light gray, medium gray, dark gray, and black) and monochromatic schemes (like white, light blue,

blue, dark blue, etc.), because moving from darker to lighter colors (or from lighter to darker colors) can indicate order and magnitude.

The bottom line is that color usually doesn't *identify* chart data, and it usually doesn't *describe* chart data. This doesn't mean that color has no place in your Excel charts. It *does* mean that chart color needs to be carefully used—unless, of course, you just want to use it as a trick to add superficial visual interest.

Another design issue relates to picture data markers, like those shown in Figure 5-24. While picture data markers are visually fun, you need to be very careful about using them because of the two charting problems they present: the problem of scaling and the problem of clutter.

The picture-data-marker scaling problem is subtle, but important. Simply stated, it's much more difficult to show your data with precision using picture data markers. In Figure 5-24, for example, the stack of dollar bills in the figure changes not just the height but also the overall appearance when you stretch and shrink it. If you stack and scale the dollar bills, you gain a little more precision, but the overall result is a loss of some visual appeal, as shown in Figure 5-26.

There's another problem with using picture data markers, too. You add a lot of detail to a chart without communicating additional information. In Figures 5-24 and 5-26, for example, the dollar bills are in and of themselves more interesting than the other data markers, but they provide no new information to people viewing the chart.

You might argue that picture data markers make a chart more interesting—at least at first glance. But, a far better way to make your chart interesting is to add substance by adding relevant data. Cheap visual gambits, which picture data markers can easily become, quickly lose their visual appeal. Interesting and relevant data does not.

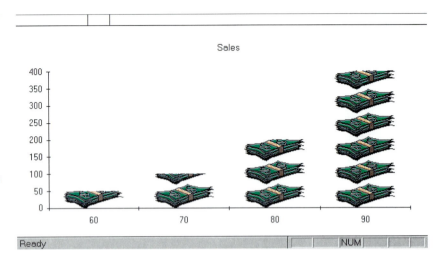

Figure 5-26: Another picture column chart. This version of an earlier chart stacks and scales dollars bills to enhance precision.

Other Formatting and Chart Design Changes

There are three other formatting and chart design changes you can make to charts displayed in their own document window. You can change the chart background. You can change the plot area. And you can change the walls and floor of a three-dimensional chart. Because these three changes all resemble each other and techniques similar to those described in earlier sections of this chapter, I'll only briefly discuss them here.

Changing the Chart Format

You can format the chart so it has a border, uses specified colors, and defaults to a particular font. To do this, you first select the chart by clicking on the chart window outside the plot area or by choosing the Select Chart command from the Chart menu. Then, you select the Patterns command from the Format or shortcut menu. When you do this, Excel displays the Patterns dialog box, as shown in Figure 5-27.

Figure 5-27: The chart area Patterns dialog box.

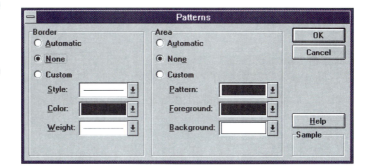

As you can guess, you use the Border settings to specify whether you want a border, or line, drawn around the chart. I've already described how the Automatic, None, and Custom radio buttons work. So, I'm going to assume you already know how they work. If you don't, just refer to the earlier discussion of changing data markers.

The Area settings control the interior of the chart. Again, I'm going to assume you're well acquainted with how these settings work, as they were discussed previously. If you have questions about how the Pattern, Foreground Color, and Background Color settings affect the chart interior, however, use the Sample picture box in the lower-right corner of the dialog box to experiment.

Changing the Default Chart Font

You can change the default font used for a chart by selecting the chart and then choosing the Font command from the Format or shortcut menu. Or, you can choose the Font command by selecting the Font command button from the Patterns dialog box used to change a chart's border and interior (see Figure 5-27). When you choose the Font command, Excel displays a Font dialog box like the one described earlier in the chapter and shown in Figure 5-9.

Changing the Plot Area

You can also make changes to a chart's plot area. Specifically, you can add a border and choose a color. To do this, you first select the chart by clicking inside the plot area or by choosing the Select Plot Area command from the Chart menu. Then, you select the Patterns command from the Format or shortcut menu. When you do this, Excel displays a Patterns dialog box that looks and works like the one shown in Figure 5-27. You can use the Border settings of the Patterns dialog box to specify whether you want a border, or line, drawn around the chart plot area. You can use the Area settings to control the interior of the chart plot area. If you have questions about how a particular pattern change affects the plot area, look at the Sample picture box.

Changing Three-Dimensional Chart Walls and Floors

You can also make changes to a three-dimensional chart's walls and floor by adding a border and changing the color. To do this, you first select the wall or floor of the chart by clicking it. Then, you select the Patterns command from the Format or shortcut menu. When you do this, Excel displays a Patterns dialog box that looks and works like the one shown in Figure 5-27. You can use the Border setting of the Pattern dialog box to specify whether you want a border, or line, drawn around the wall or floor. You can use the Area settings to control the wall or floor surface. If you have questions about how a particular pattern change affects the selected part—the walls or the floor—just use the Sample picture box.

Chart and Plot Area Changes and Chart Design

As described in the preceding paragraphs, you can change the color and the border used for the chart area, for the plot area, and, in the case of three-dimensional charts, for the chart walls and floor. Any changes you make, though, should improve readability. For this reason, you'll want to use foreground and background color combinations that contrast well with the colors used for things like the chart's axes and data markers. In most cases, white, the default color, works as well or better than the other colors in the document palette.

If you're going to produce 35mm slides, however, you will want to use a dark background such as black. and light colors for the chart's axes and data markers. Chapter 7, *Producing Chart Output*, discusses in more detail the special design issues related to 35mm slides.

Another design issue related to changing the chart format is clutter. On most cases, things like borders and drop shadows just clutter the chart. (A possible exception is when you put a chart on the same page as other textual or tabular information. In this case, it sometimes makes sense to visually segregate your chart from the other information on the page.)

Conclusion

As the words and pictures of this chapter explain, you can change almost every aspect of an Excel chart. While this flexibility might seem initially intimidating, you shouldn't have trouble as long as you keep in mind a basic tenet of good data graphics design: any changes you make should enhance the readability of your chart and increase its value.

Let me also add one final reminder. Fancy visual tricks and exotic color schemes may work well as short-term ploys to increase the visual interest of a chart, but the easiest—and, I think, the most honest—way to make your charts interesting is with interesting and informative data.

6

More on Working with Excel

The topics discussed in the preceding chapters focus on the mechanics of creating charts. This short chapter, however, takes a slightly different tack. It describes Excel application issues that relate indirectly to charting. None of the information covered here is difficult or technically complicated, by the way. It's simply stuff you'll find useful to know about Excel as you create and produce charts.

Customizing Document Color Palettes

Excel provides a 16-color palette of colors for documents, and the colors in the palette almost entirely determine which colors you can use for the charts you create. You actually aren't limited by the 16-color palette. You can choose *any* 16-colors for a palette, and you can use different palettes for different documents.

This chapter section describes, in quick order, how you go about modifying a document color palette. As you can probably guess, if the active document is a chart or a worksheet with an embedded chart, you also change the colors used in the chart.

Excel doesn't let you directly change the surface area colors of surface charts the way you can directly change data marker colors in other charts. The reason is that Excel assigns colors on a surface chart using the major value-axis units. Excel uses the third color for the first major value-axis unit, for example. It then uses the fourth color for the second major value-axis unit, the fifth color for the third major value-axis unit, and so on. Therefore, you change the colors Excel uses for a surface chart by changing the document color palette.

Changing Palette Colors

To change the colors in the palette for a chart embedded in a worksheet document, you use the Color Palette command on the Options menu on Excel's main menu bar. To change the colors in the palette for a chart document, you use the Color Palette command on the Chart menu's Charting menu bar. Either way, when you choose the Color Palette command, Excel displays the Color Palette dialog box, as shown in Figure 6-1. There are two eight-button columns. The first column of command buttons represents the first eight colors in the palette. Black is the first color, white is the second, red is the third, and so on. The second column of command buttons represents the last eight colors.

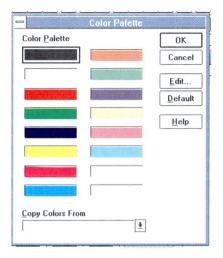

Figure 6-1: The Color Palette dialog box. Excel arranges 16 colored command buttons in two eight-button columns.

Changing a Single Color

To change one of the 16 colors in the palette, select the command button that represents the color you want to change. For example, if you don't want to use red for the third color, select the third command button in the first column by clicking it. Once you've selected the color you want to change, select the Edit command button. When you do, Excel displays the Color Picker dialog box, which you can use to define a new color. Figure 6-2 shows the Color Picker dialog box.

If your monitor isn't color, the names of the default colors rather than the colors themselves show on the Color Palette command buttons. The colors you create using the procedures described here use names like Color 1 (for the first color), Color 2 (for the second color), and so on.

You can use the Multicolored box in the upper-left corner of the Color Picker dialog box to pick a color just by clicking on a color or by dragging the color selector. This method, while easy, is also a little imprecise so Excel provides several other methods for either adjusting or specifying the color.

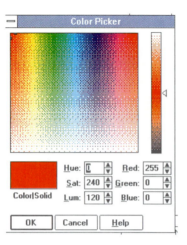

Figure 6-2: The Color Picker dialog box. The Color Picker dialog box provides several methods for changing a color.

The Color|Solid box in the lower-left corner of the Color Picker dialog box also lets you adjust colors you create using the Multicolored box. The left half of the Color|Solid box shows the actual color you've picked. The right half of the box shows the solid color closest to the actual color picked. If you want to use the closest solid color rather than the actual color picked, you can just double-click on the right half of the box.

You can adjust the luminosity, or brightness, of a color using the Brightness bar, which appears at the right of the Multicolored box. To do this, just drag the Brightness bar's arrow marker up or down. Moving the arrow up lightens the color by adding white. Moving the arrow down darkens the color by adding black. (You can also accomplish the same color adjustment using the Lum, or luminosity, text box.)

You can also specify a color by using the Hue, Sat (saturation), and Lum (luminosity) text boxes. Hue values, which can range from 0 to 239, control the shade of the color—red, yellow, green, or blue. Saturation values, which can range from 0 to

240, control the pureness of a color, or how much a color differs from gray. Luminosity values, which can range from 0 to 240, control the lightness or darkness of a color. You can, of course, change these settings by entering values in the appropriate text boxes or by clicking the arrows next to the text boxes.

You can also specify a color by mixing parts of red, green, and blue light—the primary additive colors—using the Red, Green, and Blue text boxes, because almost every color can be created by projecting some combination of these three colors. Excel creates the color red, for example, by adding together 255 parts of red, 0 parts of green, and 0 parts of blue. And it creates the color green by adding together 0 parts of red light, 255 parts of green light, and 0 parts of blue. Because the color yellow is a combination of the colors red and green, Excel creates it by adding 255 parts of red, 255 parts of green, and 0 parts of blue. White is created by adding equal parts of all the colors—in other words, 255 parts of each of the colors red, green, and blue. Black is simply the absence of any of the colors—in other words, 0 parts of each of the colors red, green, and blue.

Mixing colors by using from 0 to 255 parts of the colors red, green, and blue provides you, in theory, with more than 16 million red-green-blue part combinations and, therefore, with more than 16 million colors (256^3 = 16,777,216). You can't in practice, however, create every color in the spectrum with just these three colors. As a result, you won't always be able to produce the exact colors you want.

Using an Existing Color Palette

Once you modify a color palette and save the document, you can use that palette for other documents. To do this, you choose the Color Palette command. Then, when Excel displays the Color Palette dialog box, shown in Figure 6-1, you activate the Copy Colors From drop-down list box. The list box shows the names of all the open Excel documents. You simply select the one from which you want to copy a color palette.

Resetting a Color Palette

If you make mistakes in customizing a particular document's color palette, you can easily restore the default (16-color) palette. To do this, choose the Color Palette command so Excel displays the Color Palette dialog box. Next, select the Default command button to restore all 16 colors to their original settings. Then, select OK to implement the restored color palette.

The 16 colors in the Excel color palette won't necessarily be the only colors shown in a chart. When you copy a graphic object to a chart—for example, when you use picture data markers—Excel maintains the object's original colors.

Technical Tip

About Color Blindness

While I'm discussing the Excel color palette, it makes sense to pass along a little information about something called defective color vision—or what's commonly known as color blindness. Almost all women and most men differentiate color by mixing and matching three colors through a process called trichromatism.

However, a few women—and even more men—lack this ability. For example, some viewers need abnormal proportions of the primary colors (what's called anomalous trichromatism) to see the same colors that people without defective color vision see. Some viewers have dichromatism, which means they differentiate hues using only two primary colors. A dichromatic viewer, for example, may be unable to differentiate between reds and greens or between yellows, blues, and grays. Some viewers can even suffer from monochromatism, which means they differentiate hues using only a single color.

The problem of defective color vision may seem like a strange topic for a trade computer book, but here's the reason for bringing it up: undoubtedly, a substantial number of your chart viewers will suffer from defective color vision. For example, about eight to ten percent of men viewing a chart will have at least some trouble differentiating between red and green. Thankfully, the percentage of women with defective color vision is quite low, as is the percentage of men who have trouble with the yellow-blue-gray combinations. And, percentage-wise, very few people suffer from monochromatism. Nevertheless, remember that your charts are tools for communicating more successfully. So, you need to be sensitive to and aware of the problem as you create charts—and particularly as you make changes to a document's color palette.

Specifically, there are a couple of things you can do to mitigate the problem of viewer color blindness. The easiest way is to use colors with different luminosity. The logic for this is probably obvious: Even if a viewer has difficulty telling two hues apart—red and green, say—he or she will still be able to see the differing luminance of the two colors.

Another thing you can do is adjust one of the colors in a pair of commonly confused colors so the one color has at least a little bit of a color that's not as commonly confused. For example, red-green confusion is the most common form of defective color vision. So, to make it easier for viewers with defective color vision of differentiate these two colors, you might add blue to the green. This is, in fact, what the manufacturers of traffic lights do to make sure that color defective drivers don't have trouble telling the difference between red and green traffic lights.

Spell-Checking Chart Text

Just as you can check the spelling of the text used in an Excel worksheet, you can also check the spelling of the text used in a chart. To perform this spell-checking, you make the chart document for which you want to check spelling active. Then, you choose the Spelling command on the Chart menu. If Excel finds a word that isn't in its dictionary, it displays the Spelling dialog box, which is shown in Figure 6-3.

If the word is incorrectly spelled, you have several methods available for correcting the text. If Excel has provided an alternative spelling in the Change To text box, you can select the Change command button to correct the misspelled word. Or, if you want to change every occurrence of the misspelling, you can select the Change All command button. If the alternative

Figure 6-3: The Spelling dialog box. A word that isn't in the dictionary is identified at the top of the dialog box.

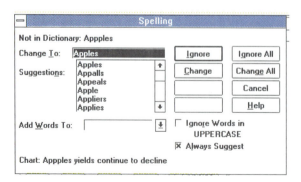

spelling in the Change To text box isn't correct, you can correct it by selecting the correct spelling from the Suggestions list box, or by typing in the correct spelling and then selecting the Change or Change All command button.

Excel attempts to provide alternative spellings for words it can't find if the Always Suggest check box is marked. If the Always Suggest check box isn't marked, you can tell Excel to look for alternative spellings by selecting the Suggest command button.

If Excel can't find a word in the dictionary but you know it's correctly spelled anyway, you can select the Ignore command button to skip past the word or the Ignore All command button to skip past every other occurrence of the word. If you want Excel to skip past words that use uppercase letters—for example, proper names—just mark the Ignore Words in the UPPERCASE check box.

You can add words to one of the Excel spelling dictionaries by identifying the appropriate dictionary using the Add Words To drop-down list box and then choosing the Add command button. Typically, you add words to the dictionary named CUSTOM.DIC, which is simply an additional list of correctly spelled words. You can also create a new dictionary. To do so, enter a name for the dictionary in the drop-down list box. The dictionary name must be a valid DOS filename, and it must use the file extension DIC.

Tip!

*Here's an important point to remember about Excel's spelling checking. When you choose the Spelling command, Excel only checks the spelling of the words in the active document. It doesn't check the spelling of words that are retrieved using link formulas, or external references. So, if the data series names are retrieved from the worksheet document with the data—the usual case—Excel doesn't check the spelling of these names. Similarly, Excel doesn't check the spelling of words in text boxes that are retrieved using link formulas from a worksheet document. Therefore, to verify the spelling of **all** the words used in an Excel chart, you need the*

Spelling command to check both the words in the chart document and the words in each of the referenced worksheet documents. On Excel's main menu bar, the Spelling command appears on the Options menu.

Protecting and Recalculating Chart Documents

Excel's Chart menu provides two other commands that haven't been discussed previously—Calculate Now and Protect Document. If you're familiar with how these two commands affect Excel worksheet documents, then you know how they affect chart documents. To be thorough, however, I'll briefly describe both commands.

As you would expect, the Calculate Now command (and its equivalent function key, F9) recalculates the formulas in all the open documents, including any open chart documents. As a practical matter, this means you can use the Calculate Now command to recalculate the worksheet document holding the data, and then recalculate the Series functions in the Chart document that retrieves the data.

The Protect Document command lets you prevent changes to the active chart and its window so that neither you nor someone else inadvertently modifies the chart. To protect the active chart, all you do is select the Protect Document command. When you do, Excel displays the Protect Document dialog box shown in Figure 6-4.

To protect the chart from additional formatting or changes to the data series formulas, mark the Chart check box. Note, how-

Figure 6-4: The Protect Document dialog box.

ever, that protecting a chart doesn't mean Excel stops updating the chart if the data points in the data series change.

To protect the chart document window from being moved or resized, mark the Windows check box. Protected chart windows can't be closed using the chart window's Control menu. You need to use the Close command on the File menu to close a protected chart window.

Optionally, you can also supply a document protection password. When a document protection password exists, only someone with the password can "unprotect" the document. To supply a password, move the selection cursor to the Passwords text box and enter the password using a combination of characters, symbols, and spaces. Excel doesn't display the password as you type, so be careful. Without the password, a document can't be "unprotected."

To unprotect a previously protected document, choose the Unprotect Document from the Chart menu. The Unprotect Document command replaces the Protect Document command when the active document is protected. If you supplied a document protection password, of course, Excel asks for the password before unprotecting the document.

To prevent embedded chart formatting and size changes, don't use the Chart menu's Protect Document command. Use the Protect Document command, which appears on the Options menu on Excel's main menu bar. When a worksheet document is protected, its embedded charts and any other graphic objects are also protected.

Tip!

You can tell Excel not to protect embedded charts and other graphic objects when document protection is enabled. To do this, select the object you don't want protected, choose the Object Protection command from the Format menu on Excel's main menu bar, and use the dialog box Excel displays to indicate you don't want the object locked with the protected document.

Setting Object Properties

In an Excel worksheet, you can control graphic objects like embedded charts, and the graphics you draw. You can also control how these objects are connected to the worksheet. To use the Object Properties command that appears on the Format menu on Excel's main menu bar when a worksheet is displayed in the active document window. When you choose the Object Properties command, Excel then displays the Object Properties dialog box, shown in Figure 6-5.

Mark the Move and Size With Cells check box if you want the selected object to move or change in size when the worksheet cells under its top left and lower right corners move. Mark the Move but Don't Size With Cells check box if you want the selected object to move but not change size when the worksheet cells under its top-left corner move. Or, mark the Don't Move or Size With Cells text box if you don't want the selected object to move or change size when the worksheet cells underneath the object move or change size.

The Print Object check box, of course, controls whether the object prints when the worksheet prints. By default, the embedded charts and graphic objects you've drawn will print.

Graphical Problem Solving

You can change data-point values stored in an Excel worksheet from chart document windows, as long as the chart type

Figure 6-5: The Object Properties dialog box.

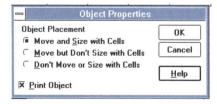

Tip!

is a two-dimensional bar, column, line, or xy chart. This feature is more significant than it might seem at first. It means you can use charts for quantitative problem solving: you can use a chart to show visually how you want a certain data set to appear. Excel goes to the work of adjusting your data set so it results in the visual picture you want.

As an example of how this all might work, suppose you created the simple financial model shown in Figure 6-6, which you want to use to calculate how quickly a new venture will generate $1,000,000 in annual sales.

Cell B2 depicts a best guess as to the initial, or first-year, sales, and it holds the value 500,000. Cell B3 shows the estimated annual growth in sales, at 12 percent. The range B5:F5 shows the years over which sales should grow to $1,000,000—1993 to 1997. Finally, the range B6:F6 holds the formulas that return the values shown in Figure 6-6. These formulas are:

B6: =+B2

C6: =+B6*(1+$B$3)

D6: =+C6*(1+$B$3)

E6: =+D6*(1+$B$3)

F6: =+E6*(1+$B$3)

Figure 6-6: A simple financial model.

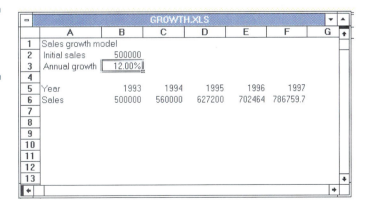

As you can see from these formulas, the first year's sales are calculated simply by referencing the initial sales input. Then, subsequent years' sales are calculated by multiplying the previous year's sales by the annual growth rate.

There are a variety of ways you might choose to plot the data in Figure 6-6, but if you wanted to concentrate on the actual data-point values, you might choose to plot the sales-revenue data in a single data-series column chart like that shown in Figure 6-7. I won't describe how you create this column chart, as you already know how to do that. It's what happens next that is interesting.

Now you could return to the worksheet model to solve this revenue problem, but you can also solve it from the Chart document window. To do this, hold down the Ctrl key and then click on the fifth year's column. Excel selects only the column and indicates the selection by adding the selection handles shown in Figure 6-8.

As Figure 6-8 shows, however, Excel not only adds the usual white selection handles that indicate the data marker can be formatted, it also adds a black selection handle to the top of the data marker to indicate that the data marker can be resized. So, you can change the height of the column by dragging the black selection handle up or down.

Figure 6-7: The sales-revenue data in a column chart. The fifth year's sales revenue still haven't reached $1,000,000.

Figure 6-8: The chart with the fifth year's column selected.

As you drag the data marker's black selection handle, Excel displays a line on the values axis to show the current data-marker value. Or, if you're dragging a data marker on an xy chart, Excel draws lines on both axes. You can't, by the way, drag the data marker above the value-axis maximum or below the value-axis minimum. So, you may need to use the Scale command to set these.

When you change the size of the data marker, Excel knows the underlying data-point value also needs to change. If the data-point value is a number stored in a worksheet cell, Excel changes the number so that the data-point value and the data marker show the same value. If the data-point value is a formula, however, Excel switches to the worksheet document and displays the Goal Seek dialog box, as shown in Figure 6-9.

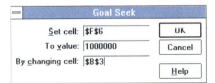

Figure 6-9: The Goal Seek dialog box. This dialog box collects the information Excel needs to begin a goal-seeking operation.

In a nutshell, what happens in a goal-seeking operation is that Excel, through a trial-and-error process, experiments with one of the inputs to a formula to find the input value that causes the formula to return the desired output value, or goal. In the case of the sales-growth model, for example, you could experiment with the annual growth-rate input in cell B3 to see how fast sales need to grow to go from $500,000 to $1,000,000 over a five-year period of time. In this case, you would enter the goal, or target value, 1,000,000, in the To Value text box. Then, you would enter the address of the cell holding the input value that Excel can change in the By Changing Cell text box, B3. The Set Cell text box holds the address of the data-point value for which you changed a data marker.

To initiate the goal-seeking operation, select OK. Excel displays the Goal Seek Status dialog box shown in Figure 6-10, as it searches for the input value that returns the target value you want. When the goal-seeking operation finishes—usually in only a second or two—the target value should equal the current value. To update the worksheet data for the results of the goal-seeking operation, just select OK. Or, alternatively, you can select Cancel, which terminates the goal-seeking operation and makes no changes to your worksheet data.

If the goal-seeking operation takes longer than a few seconds, you can suspend the goal-seeking operation by selecting the

Figure 6-10: The Goal Seek Status dialog box. The dialog box searches for the input value that returns the target value you want.

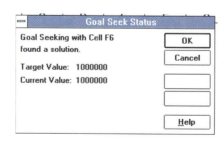

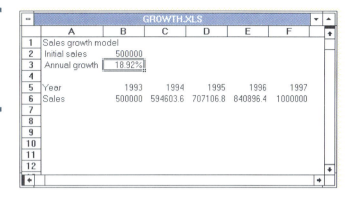

Tip!

You can use Excel's goal-seeking capability anytime you're in an Excel worksheet by choosing the Goal Seek command from the Formula menu.

Pause command button. If you've suspended a goal-seeking operation, Excel replaces the Pause command button with Continue, and you can select Continue to restart the goal-seeking. Or, if you want to continue with the goal-seeking operation but want to pause after each input value, use the Step command button.

Figure 6-11 shows the sales-growth worksheet that holds the plotted data series. The annual sales-growth rate that results in $1,000,000 in sales revenue during the fifth year of the forecast is 18.92 percent.

Conclusion

This chapter covered an eclectic set of topics, but I still think a general conclusion can be drawn from it. Simply put, it is this: to make the most of Excel's data graphics capabilities, you'll find it helpful to have a solid working knowledge of how Excel works. In fact, the more you know about Excel, the better and more professional your charts will look and the more powerful a tool you will find Excel's data graphics.

7

Producing Chart Output

Chapter 1 described the basics of printing charts that are embedded in worksheets or that are in separate chart windows. That information may be all you need if you just want are occasional charts for inclusion in hard-copy handouts for informal meetings. When you want your chart output for other purposes, however, there are several areas about which you'll want to know, including problems related to black-and white-printing, options for producing color output on paper, the mechanics of running on-line slide shows, and how to use object linking and embedding. This chapter describes each of these important chart output subjects in detail.

Black-and-White Printing

If you've read Chapter 1, you already know how to print a chart. Even with this information, however, you'll want to consider additional issues. Specifically, you want to consider how Excel converts the default colors used in a document's color palette into the black, white, and gray your printer can produce.

How Excel Converts
Colors to Black, White, and Gray

Excel uses colors from a document's 16-color palette to identify different data series or data points. Obviously, though, you can't print a color chart with a printer that uses just a single color (usually black) of ink or toner. To address this difference in capabilities, Windows converts the colors in a document's color palette to black, white, gray shades, and patterns that the printer driver for your printer allows. With the default document color palette and a Hewlett-Packard Laserjet II, for example, Windows converts the first six colors of the default palette as follows:

- *red to black*
- *green to white*
- *blue to medium gray*
- *yellow to dark gray*
- *magenta to light gray*
- *turquoise to an even lighter gray*

If you use more than six colors on a chart, Windows starts converting colors to cross-hatching patterns. For example, Windows converts brown, the seventh color, to a horizontal lines pattern, and it converts olive green, the eighth color, to a vertical lines pattern.

Figure 7-1 shows a column chart displayed on the screen using the 16-colors of the Excel color palette. Figure 7-2 shows the same column chart displayed in black and white on the print preview window. As the two figures show, it's very difficult to discern the differences in color. This is particularly so with the smaller of the data markers. As you can see, black and dark gray look nearly identical. And the graduations in brightness moving from medium gray to light gray to the lightest gray are close to imperceptible, at least to me. Even worse, though, is the moiré effect—the illusion of vibration caused by the slight tremor of the human eye—that occurs with data markers that use cross-hatching patterns.

Unfortunately, there's not much you can do about the problems inherent in printing color charts in black and white. Studies show that the human eye loses its ability to distinguish between more than about five or six shades of gray. Figure 7-2 just provides additional proof of this limit. Furthermore, unless you enjoy vibrating data markers, you won't want to

Figure 7-1: A 16-color column chart.

Figure 7-2: A black-and-white column chart.

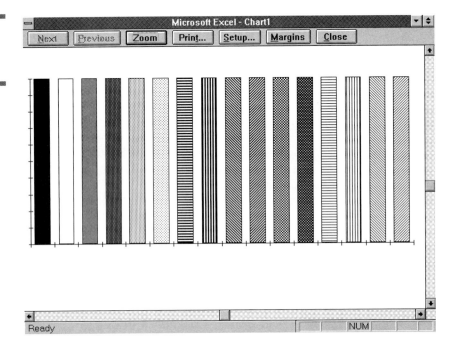

rely on the cross-hatching-for-colors conversion that Excel and Windows make.

So what's the answer? Well, if you'll ultimately print your charts in black, white, and gray, you simply need to limit the number of colors used in the chart to half a dozen or less. You can do this either by using chart types and formats that don't rely on colors—-such as line and xy charts—or by limiting the data series or points a chart shows to half a dozen items or less. (In limiting the data, what you'll usually want to do is limit the number of data series, since most Excel chart formats use color to differentiate data series.) Using either of these approaches, your charts will show only black, white, and gray shades, and none of the ridiculous, eye-straining cross-hatching patterns.

Limiting data—either by limiting the number of series or the number of data points—is particularly important when you're creating black-and-white presentation graphics like overhead transparencies. Remember that good presentation graphics are supposed to only give a quick overview of some batch of quantitative information, because the people viewing the chart don't have the time or concentration to delve deeply into the data. Remember, too, that in the case of projectors and over-head transparencies, not everyone in the audience will have a good view of the screen.

Color Output of Charts

You aren't limited to outputting Excel charts in black and white on your existing printer. You can quite easily and cheaply produce color output. In a nutshell, you have two basic choices: you can print a chart on a color printer on either paper or transparency film, or you can take a photograph of a chart and develop the film into a 35mm slide.

Color Printers

A color printer is the easiest way to produce color output of Excel charts. It's also the cheapest way to produce color out-put if you'll be producing more than just a handful of colored charts. Right now, you can pick up an inexpensive, color-capa-ble impact printer for around $300. Street prices of color inkjet printers run from under a thousand dollars to a few thousand. And, if you've got a larger budget, you may want to consider one of the more expensive color-printing technologies like thermal transfer. Prices for thermal-transfer color printers start at around four or five thousand dollars.

You may have heard that color printers are notoriously slow. Despite their sluggish speed, however, you won't usually notice the slowness all that much when it comes to printing Excel charts. The fact is that a chart, even a complicated one, is a very simple graphic with just a few lines and a handful of colored shapes.

How Color Printing Works

When your computer monitor displays colors on the screen, it actually uses three different colors of light; red, green, and blue. These are called *primary additive* colors because almost every other color can be created by projecting some combination of these three colors. Excel creates the color red, for example, by adding together 255 parts of red, 0 parts of green, and 0 parts of blue. And it creates the color green by adding together 0 parts of red light, 255 parts of green light, and 0 parts of blue. Because the color yellow is a combination of the colors red and green, Excel creates it by adding 255 parts of red, 255 parts of green, and 0 parts of blue. White is created by adding equal parts of all the colors—in other words, 255 parts of each of the colors red, green, and blue. Black is simply the absence of any of the colors—in other words, 0 parts of each of the colors red, green, and blue.

While the primary additive colors—red, green, and blue—work for creating colors when you project light, they don't work with things like ink and paint. The reason is that when you're dealing with ink, colors aren't created by projected colored light: they are created by subtracting, or absorbing, colors from the light that falls on the ink. For example, the red ink on a page of paper looks red because the ink absorbs, or subtracts, every color in the light falling on the ink except the color red.

Because things like ink and paint absorb rather than project light, a color printer doesn't use the additive primary colors red, green, and blue to create colors like your monitor does.

Rather, it uses the *subtractive primary* colors cyan, magenta, and yellow.

The subtractive primary colors are the exact opposite of the additive primary colors. Cyan is the opposite of red because it possesses every color characteristic that red doesn't and possesses none of the characteristics that red does. Magenta is the opposite of green because it possesses every color characteristic that green doesn't and none of the characteristics that green does. Yellow is the opposite of blue because it possesses every color characteristic that blue doesn't and none of the characteristics that blue does.

Because the subtractive primary colors are exact opposites of the additive primary colors, you might think that converting colors specified as combinations of red, green, and blue light to cyan, magenta, and yellow ink would be accurate. For example, you would expect that red, which is specified as 255 parts of red and 0 parts of green and blue in using light, would be specified as 0 parts of cyan and 255 parts of magenta and yellow using ink. Sounds simple, doesn't it? Unfortunately, it's not. The additive-to-subtractive primary-color conversion process isn't accurate—largely because there aren't any generally agreed upon color standards for red-green-blue color combinations. The end result of this imprecision is that charts don't look the same way printed in color as they look on your monitor. This imprecision, in fact, is the reason that the chart colors used in this book don't look exactly like the chart colors you see on your monitor.

One color that color printers using cyan, magenta, and yellow can find particularly troublesome to create is black. With only cyan, magenta, and yellow to use, a color printer creates blacks that aren't completely black, but more like a dark green. Some color printers solve this problem by adding a fourth color, black, to a color printer's color palette. Because charts use black so much—for gridlines, axis scales, text, and so on—consider spending the extra money for a printer that has not only cyan, magenta, and yellow but also black.

Color Printer Output Media

In printing color charts, you generally have a choice as to output media. Usually, you can print using regular xerographic, or "laser printer," paper or using color-printer paper that has a specially-treated print surface that more crisply and brightly displays colors. Of course, you can also usually print to transparency film such as you would use with an overhead projector. Color-printer paper and transparencies are, not surprisingly, more expensive.

There's nothing difficult about using any of these output media, however. One thing to remember is this: when you work with color-printer paper and transparencies, you'll usually need to use the Printer Setup command button on the Page Setup dialog box to adjust the print quality, because different print qualities are used for different output medias.

Producing 35mm Slides

35mm slides represent another color-chart output option. And, despite what you might think, it isn't at all difficult to create 35mm slides from Excel charts. There are just five steps to creating 35mm slides with Excel:

1. Create the chart you want to use as a slide.

2. Save the chart as a separate chart document file using the File menu's Save As command.

3. Create a high-resolution graphic image file using another graphics application such as Harvard Graphics or Power Point for Windows. (In a nutshell, the way you do this is

by importing the chart document file into a graphics application, then saving the chart as a graphic image file.)

4.   Take a picture of the graphic image of the chart using a film recorder.

5.   Develop the film into a 35mm slide.

You're already familiar with the first two steps if you've read Chapter 1, *Charting Fundamentals*. (If you aren't familiar with how to create a chart and then save it as a chart document file, refer back to Chapter 1.)

Step three, which imports a chart document file into another graphics application, is a little trickier because the precise mechanics of the file importing and graphic image file creation depend on the specific graphics application. You should know, however, that most Windows-based graphics applications will import Excel chart document files.

Usually, you'll have a slide service bureau perform the last two steps: recording the chart on film and then developing the film. Turnaround times for 35mm slides range from a few hours (if you're geographically close to one of the service bureau's branch offices or affiliates and can pick up the slide) to a day or two (if the bureau uses an overnight courier to return the slide). Prices range from $10 to $15 for a single slide, but most bureaus seem to provide varying discounts for both slide duplicates and high volumes. Table 7-1 lists half-a-dozen slide service bureaus along with telephone numbers, which you can use to contact the bureaus and find out which graphic-image file formats they support.

Tip!

You might also decide to perform the film-recording step in-house for faster turnaround time and, in some cases, cost savings. To take a picture of a graphic image chart, though, you need a film recorder. And they aren't cheap. At this writing, film recorder prices run from less than $10,000 to more than $30,000, depending on which features you want.

Table 7-1: 35mm Slide Service Bureaus

Name	Number
Autographix Overnight Slide Service	800-548-8558 or 617-272-9000
BrilliantImage	212-736-9661
Genigraphics	800-638-7348
Kinetic Presentation Centers	502-583-1679
MAGICorp	800-367-6244 or 914-592-1244
SlideImagers	800-232-5411 or 404-874-6740
Slidemasters	800-969-8228 or 214-437-0542

For more information, you can contact one of the vendors who make film recorders: Agfa Division at 800-288-4039, Mirus Industries at 800-942-9770, or Lasergraphics at 714-727-2651.

35mm Slide Design

If you decide to create slides using Excel charts, there are a couple of design points you'll want to consider. First, remember that 35mm slides have extremely high media resolution and color fidelity. For this reason, it's likely that you'll want to fine-tune any Excel charts once you get them into the graphics application that you will use to create the graphic image file.

Remember, too, that 35mm slides are small. So, with a 35mm slide, you don't have as much room for chart data. You also don't have as much room for extraneous images such as corporate logos, text boxes, and any graphic objects you've drawn.

Finally, with 35mm slides, you'll want to change the regular Excel chart coloring from dark-on-light to a light-on-dark. For example, the slide chart templates on the disk that accompanies this book use black backgrounds, and they use white and light gray for things like chart text, axis scales, and gridlines. Other light-on-dark color schemes work well, too—Yellow on dark blue, for example. Refer to Chapter 5, *Customizing Your Charts*, for more information on changing the color of a chart's parts.

Using Excel's Slide Show Feature

Excel includes an add-on utility that lets you create on-line slide shows that display a series of Excel spreadsheets and charts on your monitor. You can also use any other graphic image that can be stored on the Windows clipboard. Fortunately, though, in terms of mechanics, there isn't anything difficult about creating or using an on-line slide.

Tip!

As part of a slide show, Excel displays the "slides" of spreadsheets and charts on your computer's monitor. You may already know this, but there's also technology available to display larger images of what you see on your computer's monitor. Large screen monitors cost from $2,000 to $10,000; overhead projection panels cost from $5,000 to $10,000; and video projectors cost from $1,000 to $20,000. (All price ranges, current at this writing, are approximate.) If you want to contact specific vendors or get product specifications, just pick up a recent copy of a popular computer magazine like PC/Computing and look at the appropriate product advertisements.

Creating an On-line Slide Show

The process of creating an on-line slide show involves several steps. The very first thing you need to do is open up a slide show template file. In essence, the slide show template file simply stores the graphic images you want to display during the slide show. To open an empty slide show template, activate the File menu and then choose the New command. When Excel displays the New dialog box, as shown in Figure 7-3, select the Slides item from the list box. Then, select OK. Excel displays an empty slide show template in the document window, as shown in Figure 7-4.

To be absolutely precise, what a slide show really does is show a list of linked graphic objects along with pictures of the linked graphic objects. This technical precision doesn't matter in practice though.

Figure 7-3: The New dialog box.

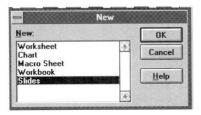

Figure 7-4: An empty slide show template.

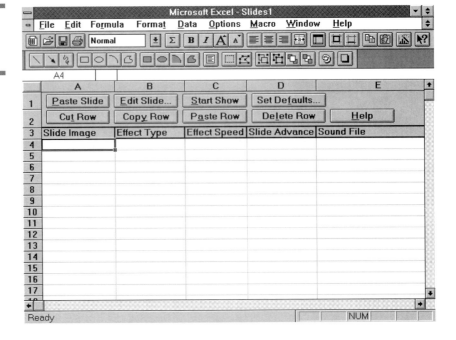

Once you've opened an empty slide show template, you add graphic images to the slide show template in the same order you want them displayed in a slide show. To add each graphic image, complete the following steps:

1. Display the document window that shows the Excel chart you want to use in a slide show. The size of the chart in the document window is roughly the same as the size of the chart that ultimately appears in the slide show, so you'll probably want to maximize the chart's document window.

2. Select the chart you want. In the case of an embedded chart, you select the range of cells under the chart. In the case of a chart displayed in its own document window, select the entire chart area, by using, for example, the Chart menu's Select Chart command.

3. Copy a picture of the chart to the Windows clipboard by choosing the Copy command from the Edit menu.

4. Display the document window that shows the template for the slide show you're creating.

5. Select the Paste Slide command button to add the graphic image currently stored on the clipboard as the next slide. Excel displays the Edit Slide dialog box, as shown in Figure 7-5.

6. **(Optional)**   Indicate which slide-to-slide transition effect you want by selecting an item listed in the Effect list box: None, Cut Through Black, Fade, Vertical Blinds, Horizontal Blinds, and so on. The effect you pick, by the way, specifies how Excel transitions from the previous slide to the slide you're adding and not from the slide you're adding to the next slide. If you aren't sure what a particular slide-to-slide transition looks like, select the Test command

Tip!

You can select an Excel worksheet range if you want to use the worksheet range as a table in the slide show.

*Figure 7-5: The
Edit Slide dialog
box.*

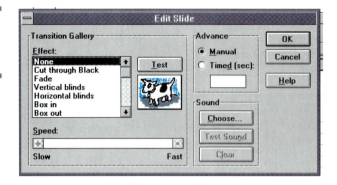

button that appears to the right of the list box. It demonstrates the currently selected slide-to-slide effect by replacing the picture of a dog with a picture of a door key.

If you scroll through the list box, you'll see that Excel provides more than 40 slide-to-slide transition effects. While you may be tempted by the length of the list, let me urge caution. First of all, conventional wisdom says you shouldn't use more than one transition effect in a presentation—and in this case, the conventional wisdom is certainly correct. What's more—and this is only my opinion—the slide-to-slide transition effects, other than None and Cut Through Black, can easily look amateurish. So, before you choose to make extensive use of, say, the Wipe Right effect, critically eye those late-night car dealership advertisements that almost surely appear on one of your local cable television stations.

7. **(Optional)** To control the speed of a slide-to-slide transition effect other than the None Effect setting, use the Speed scroll bar. (By the way, the Speed value, which shows as a number from 1 to 10, doesn't have any real meaning: it doesn't, for example, equate to some common speed measurement like seconds.)

8. **(Optional)** Excel assumes you want to manually control when it should advance to the next slide—something you do by pressing the Spacebar or clicking the mouse. If instead you want Excel to automatically advance, mark the Timed check-box and specify how many seconds Excel should display each slide using the text box next to the Timed check-box.

9. **(Optional)** With Microsoft Windows with MultiMedia Extensions or Microsoft Windows 3.1 or later, you can specify sounds you want played during the slide-to-slide transition. As with the transition effect, the sound file you pick specifies what sound Excel plays when it transitions to the slide you're adding and not from the slide you're adding. To specify which sound you want Excel to play, select the Choose Sound command button. Then, when Excel displays the Choose Sound dialog box shown in Figure 7-6, indicate the sound file you want Excel to play. Move the selection cursor to the File Name text box; enter the complete path, filename, and sound file extension, either WAV or MID; and then select OK. (If you don't know the complete path name, you can use the Drive and Directory list boxes. If you're not clear about how root directories, directories, and subdirectories are organized, refer to the *DOS Users' Guide*.)

Figure 7-6: The Choose Sound dialog box. Indicate the sound file you want Excel to play.

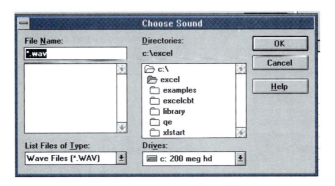

10. When the Edit Slide dialog box correctly describes the slide-to-slide transition you want from the slide you're adding to the next slide, select OK.

11. Repeat steps 1 through 10 for each of the slides you want as part of your slide show.

In the case of text and graphic images displayed by other Windows applications, such as Word for Windows, you would follow the same basic process: select the text or graphic image, copy it to the clipboard, then paste it into the slide show template.

Figure 7-7 shows the slide show template with three slides. The first cell in each row contains a picture of the slide. The second cell in each row contains the slide-to-slide transition effect: None, Cut Through Black, Fade, and so on. The second cell contains the slide-to-slide speed, with 1 representing the slowest setting and 10 representing the fastest setting. The third cell contains the slide advance setting: Manual indicates that Excel advances to the next slide by pressing the Spacebar or clicking the mouse, and a number such as 2 indicates that Excel automatically advances to the next slide after that number of seconds. If you include a sound effect for the transition, the sound file's complete path, filename, and extension appear in a row's fourth cell.

Figure 7-7: A completed slide show template. This template includes the slide-to-slide transition effect, the slide-to-slide speed, and the advance setting.

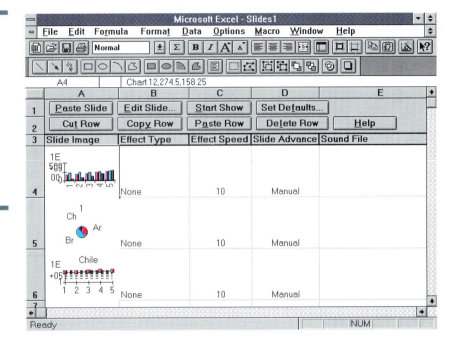

Technical Tip

Editing Slide Shows

You can make two changes to a slide show template: you can change one or more of the slide-to-slide transition effects, and you can change the order of the slides.

Changing a slide-to-slide transaction effect is easiest. You simply click on the row with the slide you want to change. Then, you select the Edit Slide command button. Excel displays the Edit Slide dialog box, as shown in Figure 7-5. You make the appropriate changes, and then you select OK.

You can also edit slide-to-slide transition effects by editing the contents of the cells that describe a particular effect. For example, if you want to change the slide-to-slide transition effect to Fade for a particular slide, select column B, or the Effect Type column, for that row, and type the effect name, Fade. To change the Effect Speed, select the column C, or the Effect Speed column, for that row, and type the effect speed number. Use the same basic approach if you want to change the Slide Advance or Sound File settings, too.

You can also change the order of the slides in a slide show simply by changing the order of the rows that hold the slide description and transition information. To perform this rearranging, you can use the Cut, Copy, Paste, and Delete command buttons.

To move a slide, for example, click on a cell in the slide's row and then choose the Cut command button; Excel removes the slide description and transition information and temporarily places it on the Windows clipboard. If you want to put the slide somewhere else in the slide show, click on a cell in the row below which you want the slide. Then, choose the Paste command button. Excel inserts a new row in the slide show and pastes the slide description and transition information into it.

To copy a slide, things work the same basic way. You click on a cell in the slide's row and then choose the Copy command button; Excel duplicates the slide description and transition information and temporarily places it on the Windows clipboard. If you want to put the slide somewhere else in the slide show, click on a cell in the row below which you want the slide. Then, choose the Paste command button. Excel inserts a new row in the slide show and pastes the slide description and transition information into it.

To remove a slide from the slide show, click on a cell in the slide's row. Then, choose the Delete command button. Excel deletes the row containing the slide description and transition effect, just as if you had used the Edit menu's Delete Rows command.

Saving a Slide Show

You save an Excel slide show the same way you save any other Excel file—with the File menu's Save and Save As commands. I won't describe here how you use these commands. If you have questions, refer to Chapter 1, which describes how you go about saving charts.

Running an Excel Slide Show

Running an Excel slide show is easy. If the slide show isn't open, you first need to open it. Then, because an Excel slide show uses object linking and embedding, Excel will ask (using a dialog box) if you want it to update the links. Select Update Refs. (I'll talk more about object linking and embedding in the next chapter section.) When Excel displays the slide show template, like the one shown in Figure 7-7, choose the Start Slides command button. Excel displays the Start Show dialog box, as shown in Figure 7-8.

To tell Excel to replay the slide show until you press Esc, mark the Repeat Show check box. To tell Excel to start with other

Figure 7-8: The Start Show dialog box.

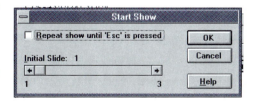

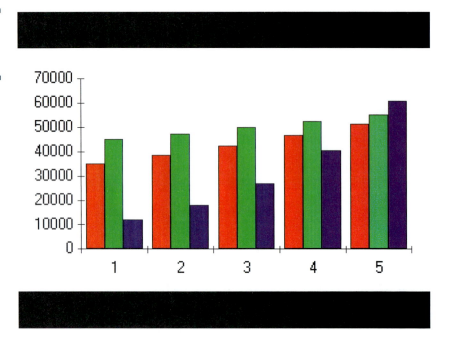

Figure 7-9: An Excel bar chart slide.

than the first slide, use the Initial Slide scroll bar marker to change the Initial Slide value to whatever slide should be displayed first. To start the slide show, predictably, you just select OK.

Excel displays the slides in the show in the same order as the rows in which they appear in the slide show template. If you specified manual slide-to-slide advancing, you'll need to press the Spacebar or click the mouse to move from one slide to the next. Figure 7-9 shows a full screen "slide show" view of an Excel bar chart.

Object Linking and Embedding

If you're using Excel 4.0 or later and Windows 3.1 or later, you should know about a special Windows capability called Object

Linking and Embedding, or OLE (pronounced oh-lay). Why? Because OLE makes it extremely easy to use Excel charts in the documents of other applications. In fact, in my opinion, the most important thing for you to know about OLE is that it's a snap to use.

With OLE, you can easily paste an Excel chart into a Word for Windows document. What's more, if the plotted data subsequently changes, Windows largely automates the process of updating the pasted chart.

To use OLE to put a copy of an Excel chart into another application's document, follow these simple steps:

1. Select the chart you want to copy by clicking on the chart or, if the chart is in its own document window, by using the Chart menu's Select Chart command. Figure 7-10 shows a simple pie chart such as you might want to copy to a written report.

2. Copy the chart by choosing the Edit menu's Copy command.

Figure 7-10: A simple pie chart.

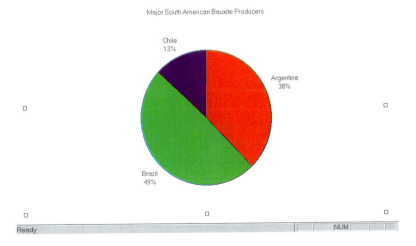

Major South American Bauxite Producers

Chile
13%

Argentina
38%

Brazil
49%

Ready   NUM

3. Start the application—such as Word for Windows—that created the document into which you want to paste chart. For example, activate the Task List dialog box, as shown in Figure 7-11, by pressing Ctrl-Esc, selecting the Program Manager from the task list, and then starting the application in the usual way. Or, if the application is already running, just select it from the task list.

4. Open the document into which the chart will be pasted. Figure 7-12, for example, shows an example Word for Windows document into which you might paste the chart shown in Figure 7-10.

5. Position the selection cursor at the location where you want the chart inserted.

6. Choose the application command that lets you paste links. In Word for Windows, for example, the command that lets you paste OLE links is Paste Special command, and it appears on the Edit menu. After you choose the paste command, the application displays a dialog box similar to the Word for Windows dialog box shown in Figure 7-13.

7. Select the first data type, Microsoft Excel Chart Object, if you want Word to embed a black-and-white picture of the copied chart from the clipboard. Or, select the second or third data types, Picture or Bitmap, if you want to embed or link a color picture of the copied chart.

Figure 7-11: The Task List dialog box.

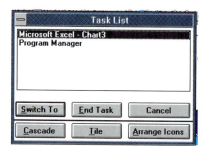

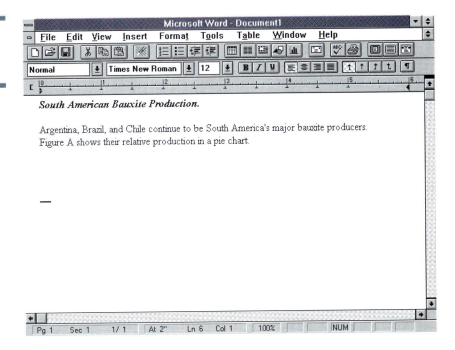

Figure 7-12: A Word for Windows document.

Figure 7-13: The Word for Windows Paste Special dialog box.

Embedded charts are simply copies of the Excel chart. Linked charts, however, are still connected to the Excel chart from which you copied them. This link has a couple of interesting effects. First, if the data changes in the chart, Windows, via the link, automatically updates the picture of the chart. Second, if you're looking at, say, the Word for Windows document but you want to see the actual Excel chart you copied, you can double-click on the linked chart. In this case, Windows displays the actual Excel chart, starting the Excel application and opening the Excel chart file if necessary.

8. To create an embedded picture of the chart, select the Paste command button. Or, to create a linked picture of the chart, select the Paste Link command button. Excel then pastes a picture of the chart into the document. Figure 7-14 shows the pie chart from Figure 7-10 pasted into the Word for Windows document.

Predictably, there's more to object linking and embedding than what I've described in the preceding paragraphs. I'm not

Figure 7-14: An embedded and linked Excel chart.

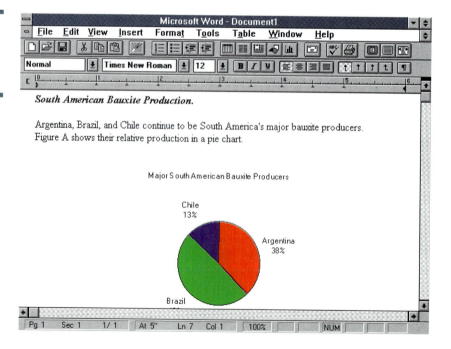

going to provide more information on the subject here, however, because the additional information you'll need to know is application specific. Accordingly, if you want more information, you'll need to refer to the user documentation for the application into which you'll be pasting Excel charts.

Conclusion

It's most likely that your Excel charts are tools you use to better communicate. Given that, it's extremely important to both explore and experiment with the methods available for presenting your charts to viewers. I've introduced you to several alternative methods of chart output here, but as always, new technologies continue to become available. And clever users—you're probably one yourself—will continue to discover and develop new tricks and techniques.

Index

Index

Index

Disk Installation Instructions

1. Put the floppy in your disk drive.

2. Make the drive active (for example, by typing A:).

3. Type PKUNZIP A:\REGULAR\REGULAR.ZIP and then the pathname of the directory where you want to install it to (for example, C:\EXCEL).

4. Follow the same instructions for the slide templates, substituting SLIDE.ZIP for REGULAR.ZIP.